How To Limit Government Spending

HOW TO LIMIT GOVERNMENT SPENDING

or how a constitutional amendment tying public spending to economic growth will decrease taxes and lessen inflation, it being in all our interest to lower outlays, provided everyone has to do it, thus increasing cooperation in society and conflict within government, which is as it should be if resource allocation is to replace resource addition as the operating principle of a government that reflects our desires not only individually as they arise but collectively over time: a good thing in itself, and better by far than mandating balanced budgets that encourage higher taxes, or imposing drastic tax cuts, which encourage inflation.

Aaron Wildavsky

UNIVERSITY OF CALIFORNIA PRESS
BERKELEY   LOS ANGELES   LONDON

This book is based on lectures presented in the Samuel S. Fels
Lecture Series on Public Policy Analysis at the School of Public
and Urban Policy at the University of Pennsylvania,
Philadelphia, in 1979.

University of California Press
Berkeley and Los Angeles, California

University of California Press, Ltd.
London, England

Printed in the United States of America

Dedication:

for Daniel Tenenberg

Contents

Acknowledgments

THIS BOOK BEGAN as the Fels Lectures at the University of Pennsylvania in the Spring of 1979. I would like to thank the School of Public and Urban Policy for giving me the opportunity and its Dean, Britton Harris, for his hospitality. The task of turning the lectures into a book was supported by the Smith Richardson Foundation; its Executive Director, Leslie Lenkowsky, was not only helpful in facilitating the proposal but also made useful comments.

My interest in this subject started with my membership on the Drafting Committee of the National Tax Limitation Committee. I benefited greatly from the discussions. My colleagues put up with a continuous stream of questions. Craig Stubblebine and William Niskanen read and commented on an early draft of the manuscript. This is a case of action generating contemplation and I am appreciative of the opportunity. Naomi Caiden, Nat Cipollina, Sidney Davidson, Robert Hartman, Allen Schick, Joseph Pechman, and Carolyn Webber tried to enlighten me on the subject. It is not their fault they only partially succeeded. I have benefited more from questions asked by members of the audience than from any other talk in my experience. There is something about the specter of the promise of expenditure limitation that turns people into political philosophers. I cannot, of course, thank my questioners by name, but I am most grateful for all I have learned from them.

[ix]

A Preface
to Constitutional
Expenditure Limitation:
Doing Together
What We Cannot Do Alone

IN SPRING 1979, in a season when hope springs eternal, following the decade of our discontent with public spending, a proposed amendment to the Constitution limiting increase in federal expenditures to the proportionate rise in Gross National Product was introduced to the Congress of the United States.[1] It is a linked limit, with each year's expenditure dependent upon the preceding year's plus the percentage of increase in the output of the nation's goods and services. Hence, under the amendment, the size of the public sector could not grow faster than the size of the private sector. Should the political process produce a lower level of spending in any one year, the level of the succeeding year, which depends on what has gone before, would similarly be lower. Emergencies declared by a two-thirds vote of Congress could increase the limit, but only a majority vote would be required to decrease it. The idea underlying the amendment was not to limit spending to some absolute amount, regardless of national productivity or of unforeseen needs, but to relate public consumption to private production so that the one would not eat up the other. A Constitutional expenditure limitation

[*1*]

is a social contract establishing a division of resources between the private and public sectors.

The long version of the amendment was proposed by the National Tax Limitation Committee, on whose drafting committee I served. The short amendment was prepared by another member, William A. Niskanen, to come closer to the usual small size and general language of amendments. Both the long and short versions (appendixes A and B) are attached to this report with accompanying commentary and data to show what the amendment can do and how its sponsors hope it will work.

Now, by way of the briefest possible introduction to constitutional expenditure limitation, I want to emphasize the difference between ordinary decisions and constitutional rules for regulating those daily choices in terms of our total expectations. The sum of our actions over time is not necessarily subject to the same considerations as our particular acts at particular times. We can (and do) want this or that expenditure now, and yet we object to the total amount of spending to which our actions have contributed.[2] Just because we have wanted it doesn't mean we like it. Unlike other creatures, like lemmings plopping into the sea, mankind is doomed to observe its own disasters; we know we are doing it to ourselves. So, for self-protection, like the dieting man who walks home without passing the bakery, we can safeguard ourselves against the temptation of eating so many desserts that we spoil the meal.

The outcome we would choose for total spending is smaller than the sum of individual items we choose to comprise it. Deciding with a total in mind is different from deciding without. Unless we all work within the same total, at the same time, however, some of us stand to get more for our favorite programs. Unless we all slow our spending simultaneously your forebearance will be my reward. In order to be free to pursue what we know is best, we must bind ourselves against our word inclinations. It is only worthwhile for me to act in my best interest if I know you are doing the same.

In a much earlier time, characterized by small size and simple sums, a direct, personal approach to excessive expenditure was possible. No official today could join in Pericles' romantic riposte on public spending:

When the oracles, who sided with Thucydides and his party, were at one time crying out, as their custom was, against Pericles, as one who squandered away the public money, and made havoc of the state revenues, he rose in the open assembly and put the question to the people, whether they thought that he had laid out much; and they saying. "Too much a great deal," "Then," said he, "since it is so, let the cost not go to your account, but to mine; and let the inscription upon the buildings stand in my name." When they heard him say thus, whether it were out of a surprise to see the greatness of his spirit or out of emulation of the glory of the works, they cried aloud, bidding him to spend on, and lay out what he thought fit from the public purse, and to spare no cost, till all were finished. [3]

Nowadays, the scope of government and the scale of spending has so far surpassed mere human dimension that only institutional artifice and constitutional remedies measure up to the size of the task.

THE PRIVATE AND THE PUBLIC SECTORS

In the beginning was the private sector. The public sector was so small it was scarcely noticeable. By the turn of this century, the experts in the public sector were "on tap," but we-the-people in the private sector were on top. Spending at all levels was just under 7 percent of Gross National Product and, within that total, the states and localities spent less than twice as much as the federal government. No more. Today federal spending has increased almost ten times (see table 1), from 2.4 to over 22 percent of Gross National Product. State and local spending is barely above half of the federal level. If money is power, relationships between citizens and government and between state and central government are not what

TABLE 1.
Federal, State and Local Expenditures in Constant Dollars (1929), 1902 to 1970*

Year	Billions of spending			Per capita spending			Percentage of GNP		
	Total	Federal	Nonfederal	Total	Federal	Nonfederal	Total	Federal	Nonfederal
1902	3.2	1.1	2.1	41	14	27	6.8	2.4	4.4
1913	5.0	1.5	3.5	52	16	36	8.0	2.4	5.6
1922	9.5	3.7	5.7	87	35	52	12.6	5.1	7.5
1932	15.4	5.5	10.8	140	44	86	21.3	7.3	14.0
1940	24.0	11.8	13.2	190	90	100	20.3	10.0	10.3
1950	46.5	28.7	17.9	307	189	118	24.7	15.7	9.0
1960	79.6	48.9	30.6	439	270	169	30.1	19.4	10.7
1970	135.5	79.8	56.7	667	389	278	34.1	21.3	12.8
1977**								22.4	

Source: Price index for 1902-22 from U.S. Bureau of the Census, Historical Statistics of the United States: Colonial Times to 1957 (Washington, D.C.: U.S. Government Printing Office, 1961); 1932-50 from Office of Business Economics (OBE), U.S. Income and Output (Washington, D.C.: U.S. Government Printing Office, 1958); 1960 from OBE, Survey of Current Business (Washington, D.C.: U.S. Government Printing Office, July, 1964); 1970 from Office of the President, Economic Report of the President, 1972 (Washington, D.C.: U.S. Government Printing Office, 1972); population data taken from Bureau of the Census, Statistical Abstract of the United States: 1971 (Washington, D.C.: U.S. Government Printing Office, 1971); government spending to 1950 from Bureau of the Census, Historical Statistics; 1960 from Bureau of the Census, Historical Statistics of the United States Colonial Times to 1951; Continuations to 1951; Continuations to 1962 and Revisions (Washington, D.C.: U.S. Government Printing Office, 1965); 1970 from Bureau of the Census, Governmental Finances in 1969-70 (Washington, D.C.: U.S. Government Printing Office, 1971); GNP data to 1960 from Bureau of the Census, Historical Statistics... Continuations; for 1970 from Bureau of the Census, Statistical Abstract... 1971.

*Thomas E. Borcherding, ed., Budgets and Bureaucrats (Durham: Duke University Press, 1977), p. 26.
**The Economic Report of the President, 1978.

they used to be. Over the years public spending has been growing much faster than the economy. Where one worker in twenty-five worked for the government in 1900, now the figure is closer to one in five. So long as you always multiply and never divide, it would take only an annual 5 percent increase in real expenditure over eighty years for total government spending to go up by 4,300 percent. Projecting this trend over two decades would bring total expenditure to nearly two-thirds of whatever is produced. The United States would change from a predominantly private to a preponderantly public country.

There are those who conclude that in the last few years federal government expenditure has not in fact increased in relation to Gross National Product (GNP). Although one might argue that a slight fluctuation over a few years does not deny the inexorable upsurge of expenditure in the twentieth century, nevertheless it is worth examining how this conclusion is reached. Renowned authorities Joseph A. Pechman and Robert W. Hartman of the Brookings Institution say that if federal outlays are counted in constant dollars, federal spending has remained at 20 percent of GNP since 1960. How has this been done? Not by mirrors but by following the convention used in the national income accounts, that there is no productivity growth in government. As a result, the trend in the federal spending share has been biased downward.[4] In ordinary language, government is alleged to have consumed less of the national product because its contribution has been systematically devalued. If this is the friendly face of government spending, it needs no ugly enemies.

There may be those who want to turn the clock back to the days of yesteryear, but they are few and I am not among them. Government has assumed larger responsibilities for social welfare and national defense without which the nation could not long continue. The question, for me at least, is not whether expenditures will take a deep dive but whether they will continue their unabated ascent. I would much rather this did not happen because, speaking personally, I think life would be much less interesting. There would be less innovation; new ideas would languish. If the costs of government were to rise, so would the size of companies who could afford to compete. There would be less variety because government guarantees collectivity, not individuality. Though I would not expect the gray uniformity of Eastern Europe, I would expect the growing uniformity that is the unvarying object of bureaucratic rules. For me, diversity is welcome. But for government, even good government, diversity is dangerous.

Considering my country, big government is no bargain. Doing what comes naturally, it will (with our consent, to be sure) eat us out of house and home. In a nation noted for the uneven development of its regions and peoples, policies that require selectivity will instead be based on homogeneity. Where race and class remain explosive issues, reducing growth in favor of giant government is unwise. Distribution of the differences would smooth social relations.

Looking at liberty, competition is its keystone. Just as science proceeds by refutation of hypotheses, and markets function by the ability to reject bids unacceptable to others, so democracy thrives on the ability to say no. We may know what we're against, as is often observed, even if we don't know what we're for. Ability to switch support, however, depends on alternatives. Being against one's own government is almost a contradiction in terms. Yet, if government is gigantic, opposition to it becomes at once essential and hopeless. Political passions rise without moderation or melioration by their ability to retreat to private preserves. If competing for control over government, as vital and honorable as that is, becomes the only game in town, incumbents of institutional power have too great an incentive to rig the rules.

Fearing for democracy, I would wish to have it well regarded. One criterion of an effective system is that it retains the best and discards the worst of the past. Yet big government adapts only by growing larger. In the language of evolutions, government selects up but not out. New programs are initiated but old ones are rarely terminated.

Another test of effectiveness is contained in John Von Neumann's ambition to create systems more reliable than any of their parts. By sending surplus resources to alleviate strain, redundancy increases reliability. By using up resources to prevent any part from faltering, by subsidizing and regulating and ensuring against diminution in emoluments for any particular segment of society, big government reduces the resilience of the system as a whole. Big government plays with Pyhrric victories. One more entitlement, a second super subsidy, security for still another lucky recipient, and it will be undone. Isn't that how we feel? After every additional protection, somehow we feel less safe than before.

Why don't I like big government? It breeds dependency, which is bad for the moral fiber of the citizenry. It breaks down, which brings disrespect. When the rate of return on government securities is higher than in the stock market, which it has been for sometime, thinking of government as one's main source of support is as understandable as it is unfortunate. In falling, as it were, by its own weight, big government threatens to take a free society with it. The liberty we prize is compromised when it appears to result in government that does too much and accomplishes too little. The disrepute of democracy is the high price we pay for elephantiasis of the political organs.

There was a time, no later than the 1950s, when liberals lusted after federal expenditure to do good. If only there were billions for higher education or for mass transportation or for mental health, on and on, what wonders would be performed! Now we know better. Government is an inadequate and expensive replacement for the family. Deep-seated behavior, requiring the cooperation of the convert, is difficult to change at any price. Those who used to argue that federal money would not bring federal effort to control education, like I did as a college student, have had their naivete exposed. It is not that public policy is good for nothing, but that it is not good for everything. And the more that is done, the more programs like disaster insurance and Medicaid lead to huge, unanticipated costs, the less we understand or are able to alter them.[5] Thus it is reasonable for us to reconsider what has been done over the decades with a view to perfecting our preferences about what we ought to want. But reconsidering and revamping public policy cannot be carried on seriously while government is expanding on all cylinders and in every sector.

Reflection before expansion. Surely this sentiment is in tune with the times. Polls of public opinion show about three-quarters of the population opposed to growth of government, even if it means cutting back on services.[6] Balanced budget amendments have been passed in thirty states. If lower spending is part of every politician's program, however, how come it never happens?

The usual approach is to consider each item of expenditure separately on its own merits. Obviously, that won't do entirely because the total might be too high on grounds of taxation or the economy. So an effort is made to establish a total within which all expenditure must fit. What is to prevent this total from simply becoming the sum of its parts? What prevents "log-rolling" where you support my spending and I support yours? Good will? Not likely; it is much easier to solve the problem of allocation by addition than by subtraction. Loss of office? Citizens want the same spending, item by item, just as they want lower totals. Unless they can take a standing decision on totals, they will continue to get what they want bit by bit, but not in total.

Few knowledgeable people believe that it will be possible to halt, for more than a year or two, the inexorable increase in spending. A sense of hopelessness surrounds the issue. When the "beasts" battle the "boobs," the sharp-toothed win over the dim-witted. Some say bureaucrats will beat us every time. Others say politicians will continue to promise and will spend themselves into office. Still others see citizens snapping up the bait of public largesse. Citizens sound like they want less public spending, the cynics say, except when it comes to their favorite programs.

Nevertheless, James Tobin, a distinguished economist, has argued that the impetus for spending on social services and income support is losing force.[7] Therefore, in his view, spending levels have reached a plateau. Demography, however, is not necessarily decisive. Spending increases not only because it is necessary but because it is possible. Like mountains, spending climbs because it is there. Why should programs and their beneficiaries do with less when they can get the government to spend more? Recognition that new proposals for spending will expand to fit any available room has led legislators who occupy important positions in the budgetary process to propose stringent limitations of their own. Explaining the conversion of House Budget Committee Chairman, Robert N. Giaimo, to legislation that would limit the government's dispensation of credit and would hold spending to a percent of GNP, the *National Journal* states, "Giaimo's change of heart springs from two sources: his opposition to new spending programs recently voted by Congress and his failure to persuade Congress to pass bills saving money in existing programs."[8] The Chairman of the Senate Appropriations Committee has followed suit. Now these proposals (there are at least a dozen other devices designed to limit spending) are legislative, not constitutional. I will explain later why I think a bill, like the one placing a ceiling on the national debt, cannot contain such strong spending pressures. But it is clear that experienced legislators, looking at their inability to resist huge, new expenditures outside the regular budget, such as those resulting from the windfall tax on oil, are coming to favor stronger self-limitation.

If I thought the ordinary operation of the existing political process would lead to less expenditure, I would not be advocating a constitutional amendment limiting the rise in public spending to a proportionate increase in private production. If I thought democracy were doomed, if nothing could stop society from being absorbed into government, I would not bother. Why do I believe constitutional expenditure limitation will help us do together—to prevent the public sector from growing at the expense of the private—what we are currently unable to do alone?

At a recent round table on budgeting, an experienced auditor said that the purpose of standards was to allow weak-minded auditors to resist pressure by saying, "I can't do this." He was followed by a practitioner of budgeting who said that the prospects for reducing spending depend on three things: (1) the principle of equal sacrifice; (2) an inability to pass the buck; and (3) a gradual rather than a precipitous reduction in expectations of service. All of these purposes would be accomplished by the amendment. Because there is a fixed ceiling that everyone knows will last a long time, constitutional limits prevent passing the buck; since spending is allowed to grow absolutely, being limited only relative to national product, there need only be a gradual reduction in expectations of indefinite increases; and because great growth in some programs will, by virtue of limitation, require a corresponding reduction in others, self-interest will help supervise equality of sacrifice.

The major objection raised by knowledgeable people is that if the federal budget is blocked, spenders (always more numerous than savers) will make end runs around it. The trouble with this argument is that what the predicted consequence of limitation has already happened without it. At this very minute, in addition to a federal budget of over $600 billion, there exists around $30 billion of off-budget spending by quasi-governmental corporations, $100 billion of spending through the tax process, and a whopping $440 billion of guaranteed credit. What our good budget boys will do when they are naughty I dare not imagine.

IRONIES OF EXPENDITURE LIMITATION

A nice irony of expenditure limitation is that it will lead to a 180 degree reversal of current political postures. Conservatives argue that social processes in which individuals are left to pursue their own interests (under agreed rules facilitating the flow of information and freedom of choice) will produce better results than would central command. Liberals say that governmental intervention is essential to overcome the hidden hierarchies of market manipulation that perpetuate inequality. Constitutional expenditure limitation will lead each side to adopt the arguments of the other.

In politics, like markets, good decisions are those on which there is agreement, not those deemed correct according to cogitation by a wise man sitting astride the relevant hierarchy. Yet the "invisible hand" that is supposed to guide markets must be missing in politics. Otherwise conservatives would not want to intervene, so to speak, with a constitutional club. For their part, I predict that liberals (in the pristine sense of the word signifying largesse and liberality, that is, more spending) I will postulate a hidden intelligence assuring optimal political outcomes. They must; otherwise they will be unable to argue against those meddlesome social experimenters who will tamper with the wondrous work of the founding fathers. The liberals will argue that the political process, left to its own devices, will arrive at expenditures, both individual and total, that are more appropriate than if these decisions were prejudged by being fit into a procrustean constitutional limit.

The proponents of expenditure limitation argue the opposite: individual expenditure decisions do not add up to what citizens would choose collectively, were they given the choice. Each part of public expenditure is wanted; only the whole is unwanted. *Bringing the two types of decisions together—totals over time and particular parts one at a time—is the essence of expenditure limitation.*

Keeping the parts and the whole separate is the essence of an unstated liberal-conservative alliance on high spending. Conservatives fear defense will not win; liberals fear welfare will not win; so they tacitly decide not to impose or abide by spending limits. As things stand, both sides get what they want, higher defense and welfare spending. It is only the country that loses.

The amendment places a ceiling on spending but not a

floor. Some of its sponsors hope that eventually expenditure will comprise a significantly lower proportion of GNP than it does now. I doubt it. Whatever is known about spending suggests that ceilings also become floors. Too many people want too much from government to get less than they can. Even the increase in spending that provokes public protest is evidently insufficient for its proponents or else they would not seek to circumvent existing budgetary procedures. Conservative congressmen will discover that it is easier to keep constituents happy and to reconcile diverse interests by spending up to (or just below) the limit. As soon as they realize that lowered spending for one year shrinks the base for the next, they will be reluctant to tie themselves down. We will be fortunate enough to keep within the limit without projecting fantasies about lowering it.

There is a circumstance, however, under which spending could decline substantially as a proportional part of GNP. The long amendment contains a provision penalizing expenditure during inflationary periods. For every 4 percent increase in inflation (above the first 3) a 1 percent decrease in spending is mandated. The government would no longer have more to spend during inflation, as it has today. The government would have every incentive to prevent inflation.[9]

Politically impossible; this is when presence would be greatest to curtain spending

BALANCED BUDGETS MEAN HIGHER SPENDING

Though it does not mandate a balanced budget, by relating expenditure to national product, which in turn is related to revenues, the amendment should achieve that result on a decade-by-decade basis. (Applying the amendment retroactively, as in appendixes A and B, suggests that the budget would have been nearly balanced over the past decade. Of course, it is not possible to know what would have happened had other policies also changed.) While balance over time is desirable, and I am sympathetic to those who want to bring revenues and expenditures closer together, I am not in favor

TABLE 2

BUDGET PROJECTIONS—FISCAL YEARS 1978 TO 1984*

Amount (billions of dollars)		
Fiscal year	Receipts	Outlays	Margin

Administration estimates			
1978	402.0	450.8	-48.8
1979	456.0	493.4	-37.4
1980	502.6	531.6	-29.0
1981	576.8	578.0	- 1.2
1982	652.6	614.9	37.8
1983	718.3	645.6	72.7
1984	780.2	673.7	106.5

Congressional Budget Office assumptions			
1978	402.0	450.8	-48.8
1979	454.6	493.5	-38.9
1980	499.4	540.0	-40.6
1981	582.0	590.6	- 8.6
1982	674.7	641.5	33.2
1983	761.7	688.5	73.2
1984	860.4	734.1	126.3

Sources: *The Budget of the United States Government, Fiscal Year 1980*, pp. 35-36, and authors' estimates.

*Adapted from Joseph A. Pechman and Robert W. Hartman *in* Joseph A. Pechman, ed., *Setting National Priorities, The 1980 Budget* (Washington, D.C.; The Brookings Institution), p. 46.

of balanced budget amendments because they are at once too rigid and too weak. Their rigidity prevents varied spending and taxation for counter-cyclical purposes. Their weakness permits any level of spending, however high, so long as it is matched by revenues. I want to stop government growing larger than the rest of us, not encourage government to take more from us.

The impetus a balanced budget amendment would give to increased federal spending becomes clear from a perusal of estimates (see table 2) of tax receipts in the early 1980s. By

1984, for example, the Office of Management and Budget estimates receipts at $780 billion and the Congressional Budget Office estimates receipts at $860 billion. This compares with $503 billion in 1980. This is how a deficit of some $29 billion in 1980 gets converted to a surplus of over $100 billion in 1984. With inflation pushing taxpayers into higher brackets, the mobilization of resources permits the 1980 expenditure of $532 billion to rise to $674 billion and $734 billion by 1984, depending on which estimate is more accurate. A license to spend is not what we want.

Balanced budget amendments also fall afoul of the rule of parsimony and the injunction against temptation. Limitation of any kind will be difficult enough without trying to control twice as much. Adding tax to expenditure limits will create twice as much work and two times as many enemies without achieving as good results, as we shall see. Spending limits will inexorably lower tax rates and will achieve budget balance over time without opening up new loopholes. By working with revenues as well as with expenditures, for instance, the manipulation of estimated tax receipts joins the list of ploys by which expenditure may be increased without appearing to be so. In the case of the balanced budget, two temptations (on the revenue as well as the spending side) are worse than one.

Nevertheless, balanced budgets are better than instant, drastic tax cuts of the kind advocated by Howard Jarvis in California's new (1980) Proposition 9. The proposed 50 percent decrease, aside from feeding inflation, will breed disrespect for government, which ought not be forced to phase out so many activities all at once. A slower step-by-step reduction would come about in any event. On the taxing side, legislation already indexes it to income; on the spending side, the Gann Amendment already ties spending to state income so that as productivity grows taxes will decline in proportion. A gradual approach is much more likely to last if there is time for adjustment so that claims of irreparable damage do not lead to breaches in the entire edifice. Every movement has its burden to bear. Proposition 9—Jarvis II (or "Jaws II," as it is affectionately known)—is ours.

Why does the amendment limit outlays rather than appropriations or, for that matter, revenue rather than expenditure? Though appropriations are forward-looking, which is desirable in setting prior limits for later spending, they are also fissiparous, which is undesirable, In short, appropriations leak; they are full of holes. Some appropriations are "open-ended" and others are "continuing," meaning that the amounts they contain or the time during which they can be paid out (or both) is unspecified. What is worse, off-budget outlays by quasi-independent bodies are not counted as appropriations in conventional usage and thus are not subject to limits. Predictably, use of off-budget entities in order to circumvent expenditure limits would be irresistible. The concept of outlays includes both on- and off-budget spending.

If limits were to be imposed on outlays, a practitioner of public spending would raise the question of how large projects requiring years of effort, like dams or buildings, would be administered. Today, funds are obligated early and spent late as costs are incurred. Tomorrow, under expenditure limitation, each year's expenditures would belong to it. Other proposed spending would have to be cut to make room. Is that fair? Is that efficient? If we were dealing with one project at a time, the difficulty might be insurmountable. But the vast number and variety of federal projects suggests that total spending would smooth itself out. Should experience suggest otherwise, any imbalance could be corrected by creating contingency funds. These would be subject to the limit during the year they were put aside, but they would be outside the limit in subsequent years. Instead of spending in the present, which increases spending in the future (as is currently the case), each year would be encouraged to look after itself. Thus, on a year to year basis, spending would be stabilized.

What effects on economic management, by contrast, would accrue from expenditure limitation? Slowing down the economy by decreasing spending and increasing taxation to create a surplus should create no new difficulties. Whatever was done yesterday could be done tomorrow. The difference would be that lower expenditure one year would reduce the limit for the next, so that it would be correspondingly more difficult to increase spending. Going the other route, however, by creating a deficit to stoke up the economy, cannot be done in quite the same way. Spending can be pushed to the limit but, as we know, not beyond. This means, in a severe situation, that tax reduction to create a deficit must bear the brunt of "priming the pump." The question is whether reliance on raising or lowering taxes should be the mainstay of budget policy in attempting to manage the economy? Except in the instance of a depression, which could be countered by spending permitted under the emergency provisions, spending could be counterproductive to smoothing out economic fluctuations.

Given a choice, I would prefer the usual route by which proposed constitutional amendments are submitted to the states by Congress for ratification. But I believe that the attempt to undermine budget balancing on the grounds that a convention called by the states would not confine itself to spending (the image of wholesale revision amounting to revolution) is a scare tactic. The likelihood of convincing so many state delegations, chosen for their interest only in this issue, to coalesce on a new consitution is low enough. The joint probability of delegates agreeing on constitutional changes and of having them approved by state legislatures in three-fourths of the states approaches zero. (Indeed, if negative numbers were acceptable, I would use those.) Should this method be the supreme objection, Congress could propose the amendment itself. The positive point of this argument is that it has made the proposed amendment appear more moderate in comparison with those "barn-burning budget balancers," if I may be permitted more than the usual hyperbole. But this perception, like the fear of a runaway convention, is entirely misplaced. The amendment limits expenditure far more stringently than one permitting (or encouraging) taxes to rise so as to accommodate higher expenditure.

ADVOCACY AND SKEPTICISM

The amendment is not a mere technical improvement in budgeting. It does more than limit expenditure. The amendment is a budget of budgets. If it did not affect outcomes—who gets how much for what—there would be no reason to bother. Grand choices are up for grabs, so it is prudent to proceed with care.

I am an advocate, but I have also tried to be a skeptic. Many difficult questions should be answered before a reasonable person would want to support an amendment to limit federal expenditure. Is it desirable to amend the Constitution or to limit federal spending? Why not rely on the political process? Why limit the flexibility of future generations? Why read an economic doctrine into the Constitution? Why tamper with a procedural document that has achieved widespread acceptance precisely because it does not take sides on public policy? These questions I shall answer in the affirmative. Whether or not my arguments are ultimately convincing, I hope to persuade everyone that these are good questions because they open up fundamental queries about how the American political system has been transformed by the rise of big government and what, if anything, should be done about it. In over two decades of lecturing, I have never found a topic as productive of profound questions as that of limiting expenditure by constitutional amendment.

In the first lecture, I will argue that the amendment is desirable if (admittedly a big "if") it works as advertised. In the second, third, and fourth lectures, I will explain why these difficulties have not arisen in the past, why we are all responsible and how amending the Constitution can create a rule for decision on expenditure that will bring our individual choices into line with our desires for total spending. Then, in lectures five and six, in order to see whether the amendment will stand up, I shall marshall the strongest arguments—inefficacy and immorality—against constitutional limitation of expenditure.

Even if it were desirable, the amendment might not be workable. Would a constitutional amendment limiting federal expenditure to its existing amount plus the percentage increase in dollar GNP be efficacious? A skeptical suspension of judgment is in order. Getting around the amendment —by increasing tax expenditure (reducing taxes if the money is spent for particular purposes), or by imposing costs on the private sector (such as mandating health insurance or environmental protection), or by guaranteeing credit (already at astronomical levels)—might lead the nation to spend more in stupider ways than before. If increase in GNP can be expanded by sleight of hand, or if receipts can be subtracted from outlays, or if other devices can be used to circumvent its intent, expenditure limitation may be another wonderful idea whose time should never come.

Ways of subverting

Even if it were workable, the amendment might not be desirable. Any constitutional amendment should benefit most citizens, not just a favored few. If the amendment were shown to favor the rich over the poor or white against black, or, more generally, the have-much over the have-little, it could not command our respect. The place to begin is not with the amendment itself but with the nation's experience with big government. If the experience were satisfying, there would be no need to guarantee ourselves less of a good thing. Because this experience is recent—barely twenty years old— it is not surprising that at the beginning neither the nation nor its government knew all there was to know about public policy. By proposing to surround liberal social policies with conservative spending constraints, constitutional expenditure limitation shows that we are beginning to learn.

This book, I believe, has use for those who disagree as well as those who agree with my position. For those who are sympathetic, the book explains why they might wish to limit expenditures to a proportion of GNP and also makes them aware of pitfalls in their own positions. People inclined to oppose this proposition at the current time should look toward the day when they may wish to make use of the insights offered here. Even if they do not wish to limit expenditures today, they may wish, from a different political perspective, to limit them tomorrow.

Let us assume that European social democrats, committed to the welfare state, wish to see expenditures rise to 50 or 60 percent of GNP. Whether they believe with Ray Jenkins, the President of the European Community and former Labor Party Minister in Britain, that much over half the national effort would make a pluralist society impossible, or whether they merely wish to assure a high but steady state of social expenditures to maintain political support, they must eventually face up to the need for a limit beyond which public spending should not go. How, then, will they maintain this limit? What will they do if expenditures keep climbing? They also will have to ask why spending grows, and why ordinary methods of item-by-item control have not worked. They will also have to ask whether, without a total fixed in advance to which everyone is subject, any interest will make the required sacrifices. Whatever they say now, American welfare state liberals and European social democrats will eventually have to get their act together on public spending. Sooner or later, probably sooner, this book will be relevant for them, too.

The student of public spending, I believe, whether interested in limitation or not, will find herein a useful perspective. I thought I knew something about budgeting, but asking why expenditures keep rising, asking what would happen if there were a constitutional limit, has enriched my understanding. Much that was obscure, not only in the literature on spending but in my own prior work, has been clarified. Asking "what if...?" is a good way to break up rigid patterns of thought. Back of this examination of public spending is a reexamination of what is wrong with the way we have thought about and practiced budgeting.

1

Introduction:
Progress and Public Policy

IN THE 1960s America fell in love with the Rachel of social reform but found itself married to the Leah of big government. She was bigger but she wasn't better. It proved more inspiring to desire the unobtainable objectives of giant governmental programs than to wonder if they were worth having. Overinfatuated with the good they sought to do, Americans overemphasized the evil they had done. The idea of progress in public policy was, if not speedily seduced and abandoned, at least slowly suspended and perhaps discarded. Unrequited love easily turns on its object. Along the way, characteristic American optimism was subject to severe shock. Retrogression rather than progression became the expectation. Why?

Americans were better educated, more talented, richer in human and material resources than ever before. Their sense of social justice, though far from perfect, was certainly sharper than in earlier times. Challenged to put up or shut up, they opened their coffers so wide as to shame a Croesus. Whereas in the early sixties, defense took up some 45 percent of the federal budget and social welfare programs some 20 percent, a scant decade later these proportions and priorities were radically reversed. Relatively and absolutely, social welfare, from food stamps to Medicaid to social security, loomed larger on the government horizon.[1] Why, then, weren't we-the-people happy? Why did we recoil from our fondest hopes, damning what we had so earnestly desired?

Actually, it hasn't been all so bad or so consistent. Some social programs have retained support. Had they not, they would not be with us. Even so, the elan, the enthusiasm, the pure pleasure, the expectation of better things to come has gone. Wariness has replaced happiness. If the nation entered the seventies celebrating the change from warfare to welfare, it is exiting on a note of retrenchment. Thirteen has become the lucky number for advocates of lowered local real estate taxes in California; balance in public policy no longer signifies doing more to help the poor but restricting government spending. What has happened?

This book advocates a constitutional amendment to limit the increase in public spending to a proportionate increase of private production, but it does not negate the notion of public life. It does not reject the sixties or castigate public policies to aid the poor. Not at all. I do not believe that the sixties was a dreadful decade. No people are wise to abandon their past, pretending it did not exist, or preferring it had taken a wholly different path (unless, of course, it was vile and mean spirited, which ours was not).

For good or ill, our culture is self-conscious. We transport ourselves to the corners of our living rooms and observe our own behavior, subject and object together. We have no choice but to try to learn from our mistakes. If error recognition is the essence of rationality, and error correction is the essence of right action, then we have had plenty of opportunity to learn in the school of public policy.

Learning incorporates rules for retaining the best and discarding the worst of old solutions while testing new ones. Constitutional expenditure limitation is one such rule. It establishes restraints that prevent stockpiling of solutions (old and new, good and bad), and constraints within which all have to compete, because not all can survive at the same level. In order to understand why this amendment appears at the present time, it is essential to review recent public policy, to which this action is a reaction. When we better understand what has happened to the idea of progress, we will better connect past and future, infusing progress in public policy with the potential for something more than growth.

THE MALAISE OF PUBLIC POLICY

Big government, which was supposed to institutionalize progress in public policy, has instead become identified with retrogression. There is little confidence that "doing more of the same" or "throwing money after problems," to use two of the current stock phrases, will make things better, and there is much confidence that even bigger government will make them worse. At first this reaction seems surprising, because those social welfare programs that have grown the fastest in the last two decades were introduced as modes of progress—sharing the wealth of the private sector through redistribution by the public. Whereas the private sector was fueled by self-interest, the public sector was said to be motivated by moral concern for the disadvantaged. A heightened awareness of duty to others less fortunate, a more exquisite moral sensibility, was expected to marry the wealth of society to the government's efficient allocative capacity to do good. Obviously, something happened on the way to public happiness.

On second thought, it is not surprising that something so new, too much too soon, stumbled at the start. In view of our inexperience, it would have been extraordinary to discover that programs performed as intended, that each reinforced rather than crossed purposes with the other, so that social difficulties declined. Temporary dismay at the decline of high hopes is easy to understand; permanent disappointment leading to demands for dismantling the system of social welfare makes sense only if government is fatally flawed. This kind of criticism does not come from the right but the left.

PROGRESSION VERSUS PROGRESS

The concept of progress (a radical innovation for its time) was coined by Condorcet to counter the nostalgic notion of a beatific past from which time all has gone downhill. The "golden age" was not so much a has-been as a never-was. No need to worry, however, for education would sweep away the vestiges of the past. By overcoming prejudice and superstition, indeed by understanding scientifically the principles of society, mankind could continuously improve. Education and science have been considered important prerequisites to progress, but from that day to this the idea of progress has had hidden ambiguities about process and purpose that we wish to explore.

It was comforting, to be sure, that all kinds of progress went together—material, moral, and mental. Earlier traditions, imbued with the doctrine of original sin, were likely to view the will as the servant of the passions, and both as directing the weaker moral and material orders. Earlier also was a view of cycles that societies passed through but did not transcend. Change was permanent but betterment was not. Rise and decline were related; as politicians climbing the slippery hill of success have observed, the first step up is also the first step down. Man, who has labored ceaselessly, is more like Sisyphus than Prometheus.

Without religion, without the justification of this life by an afterlife, the ultimate purpose of progression—life as history and history as dates—was unsettled. Whether there was to be evolution or revolution (or both) in this world, whether its saint was to be Darwin or Marx, the question of motivation remained. The need was particularly poignant under Marxism, because it promised to liberate mankind not only from

supersitition but also from need. How would people arrange
their lives, what would motivate them when they no longer
had to work? If there were a secular side to motivation, it had
been tied to the conversion of history into meaning, that is,
of progression into progress.

Progress was bolstered by evolution. Here was not merely
a prediction of glad tidings, but a method assuring believers
that the best had been chosen by natural selection, assuring
survival of the fittest. What Protestant predestination did for
the moral universe, evolution justified for the material world.
From the beginning, however, there were doubters and dis-
believers who thought it was all too neat.

Was there survival of the fittest, or did those who survived
call themselves fit? Was there, in short, progress or only
power in disguise? That one thing succeeded another was
undeniable; but was succession (the day-to-day affluvia of
historical deposits) success? Religion left ultimate goodness
to God, the last things appearing in all their perfection after
history was over. For those who lived in history, however,
the question remained: was it a random series of events or
was there a successful social mechanism for discarding the
worst and selecting the best?

Summing up this tour of the horizon of ideas about progress, we see that men of the Enlightenment believed that by
stripping away the myths and superstitions of the past and by
replacing them with an education based on science, mankind's essential morality would be set free. Enlightenment
was then supplemented by evolution. To the learning of individuals was added the wisdom of the species. Each individual
would benefit from the knowledge of others, about which he
could not (and fortunately did not need to) know. There was
coordination but no coordinator. Some of the newly enlightened saw a benevolent social intelligence at work in the economy, so that private interests willy-nilly produced public
good. Others placed this ultimate design in government,
where espousal of public interests led to private good. The
contradiction has never been resolved.

Government was supposed to grow not only quantitatively but qualitatively. The significance of evolution was that it postulated a process for selecting good programs and discarding bad ones. That sheer size might cripple quality was not considered, for with size went wealth. The growth of government was presumed to proceed apace with (not apart from) the growth of society.

In the past, partisans of progress expected risk to be countered by resilience. Each generation would not only be richer than the one before, it would also be more resilient in the face of new challenges. It was not necessary, therefore, for each generation to pay all the costs of rapid technological change. These could be left to the future on the assumption that it would be more capable. Without faith in progress, without the belief that deficits would be made up by development, few would have ventured so far so fast. All of these conditions of progress as it has been understood—education, selection, growth, resilience—have been subject to severe challenge by experience with big government.

BIG GOVERNMENT AND LITTLE PROGRESS[2]

By "big government" I mean government that is large historically relative to the private sector and large absolutely compared with past programs. The increase in number of programs is significant, both in terms of diversity and of impact on people's lives. Difficulties may arise along any of these dimensions.

Think of public programs as spheres existing in policy spaces. When these spaces are unoccupied, new programs have only their own consequences to consider. As these programs grow larger and are joined by others, they bounce off of one another. The larger the number of big programs, and the more they bang into others, the more varied and indirect their consequences become. A new income maintenance program, for example, will have far-reaching effects on housing, consumption, transportation, medical care, and so on. The result is that complexity overcomes theory. Ability to control consequences by program design diminishes as unanticipated consequences increase. The point is that even as available knowledge accumulates at a steady pace, the knowledge needed for large programs in big government grows by leaps and bounds. There is progress in understanding but retrogression in public policy.

Past progress, moreover, creates future problems. Just as yesterday's pneumonia victim is today's geriatric problem, overcoming easy difficulties may leave government stuck with intractable problems. Today's medical inflation is a direct result of subsidizing hospital construction, pouring money into Medicaid and Medicare, encouraging medical insurers to push comprehensive coverage, and otherwise flooding the medical market with money, thereby driving up prices. New programs—cost containment, second opinions on surgery, restriction of hospital beds, on and on—become necessary in order to cope with past consequences. When programs get big, involving millions of people and billions of dollars, they become such a large part of their sectors that, by their very presence, they alter its outcomes.

The larger government grows, the more policies become their own causes. The more government does, the more it needs to fix what it does. The larger government gets, the less it responds to events in society and the more it reacts to the consequences of its past policies. In an era of big government, policies increasingly become their own causes.

Just as any football coach knows that victories are in part a function of scheduling weak instead of strong opponents, the capacity to control public policies depends on what one tries to do. The justification of big government must be that it does grand things. The upshot is that government undertakes tasks that no one knows how to accomplish—raising the cognitive abilities of deprived children, reducing crime and recidivism rates, improving health. No matter how much money is spent, reading, health, and recidivism rates do not improve, because there is no known way of doing these things. (By the way, Europeans are no more successful than Americans; they just don't advertise their failures as much.) A characteristic feature of all such programs is that change resides within the individual, not within government. Where governments seek to change their own behavior, the variable over which they have the most control, they sometimes succeed. The radical reorientation of priorities from defense to social welfare is evidence of that. (Defense was about twice as large in 1960, and by 1975 the relationship had been reversed.) But where government seeks to alter deep-seated human behavior, it often fails. Health, education, and welfare speak eloquently on this subject.

If it cannot do what it says, what does big government do? It does what it can. Government governs by inputs—the resources it controls. It pours money over problems as a sign of good intentions. It reorganizes itself endlessly. It tries everything at least once and some things, like tying welfare to work, many times. This is how the widespread impression of change for its own sake is created.

When programs do not work at all or as well as they might, efforts at error detection and correction are expected. Efforts there are, but accomplishment is a sometime thing. Actually, error correction goes on all the time, but the solution is almost always larger than the problem.

If evolution were accompanied by devolution, the size of problems might be reduced to an intelligible scope. And if evolution took place in the midst of competition, the politically or economically fittest might survive, leading to public approval. Instead, what you see is what you get: the Dinosaur Syndrome operates so that every solution increases the size of programs without simultaneously increasing the intelligence of those who design and administer them.

Size turns out to be incompatible with equality. The original motive behind welfare policy—redistributing income to increase equality—is at odds with increasing size. Why this should be so is one of those observations that is perhaps too obvious to be noticeable. When programs originate, they are designed to meet a need. A relatively small group is targeted to receive aid. Since the cash comes from the general population of taxpayers, people of plenty, so to speak, are paying for the poor. This is how programs begin but not how they end. Either the original beneficiaries want more money or previously uncovered groups want to be included. The way to do this, which adds to initial support, is to have larger benefits for a broader array of people. When this process has run its course, however, many more beneficiaries from more diverse social groups are receiving higher levels of benefits. The people paying and the people receiving, though they are by no means identical, have come to resemble each other much more than they did before. Naturally, when proponents of redistribution check out these programs, they discover that their early egalitarian impulses have been much attenuated. The broader the social base and the higher the benefits, the less egalitarian the program. The end result is that though ever larger amounts are spent on ever larger numbers of recipients of welfare programs, there is less reduction of inequality.

This size syndrome operates according to well-known principles. Small errors are easy to correct but difficult to detect, because it is hard to trace consequences to a multitude of possible causes among innumerable governmental programs. Large errors are easy to detect but difficult to correct, because so many people and programs are connected to them that the effort appears disproportionate to the result.

How is opposition to large scale change, requiring numerous adjustments in related programs, overcome? Decreasing size worsens internal competition by setting off a struggle for resources. The trouble with competition is that one can lose. Increasing size has happier internal consequences; everyone gets more as change is exchanged for growth. The inexorable collective consequence is giant government.

Now we know why, in a period of enlightened social programs when huge sums are spent to right social wrongs, the prevailing view of public policy is best described as progression (one thing does lead to another and bigger thing) but not as progress. Solutions create new problems faster than they solve old ones. Problem creation overtakes problem solution. Knowledge required to control public policy grows geometrically, while understanding of public policies increases only arithmetically. The ability to measure failure (evaluation) leaps ahead of the capacity to cause success.

Since people who give consent to public policies are often the same ones who are unwilling or unable to change their own behavior, they have every reason to know that particular programs are not working. Citizens see that selection has given way to collection. The Dinosaur Syndrome dominates government, an impression reinforced by evidence of incapacity to respond flexibly and precisely to crises. The tail of government is so heavy, its programs are so interdependent, that selective intervention is awkward and massive action is ungainly. Energy is a good example (the current policy being to undo what government has done in controlling prices) of the cure being worse than the original disease. The paradox of progress is that while most things (with the exception of crime) are getting better for most people, they perceive that government is getting worse.

MAKING PROGRESS POSSIBLE

There are two ways to do better—change the criteria and improve performance—and I propose we do both. The idea that problems are solved should give way to the notion that man-made solutions also create man-made problems. Policies don't succeed so much as they are superseded. It is not policy resolution but policy evolution that should be our concern. How well, we should be asking, have we detected and corrected our errors? More to the point, are we better able to learn from today's errors than we were from yesterday's? If, in an era of big government, the question radiates with doubt, a partial answer may be to introduce competition for limited resources so as to revive selection and to reinvigorate resilience.

Thinking of social ills as puzzles that can be solved instead of as problems that may be alleviated or eventually superseded tends to make us despondent when they do not yield to our ministrations. For example, when we do something and evaluate the result, we don't know whether some other action might have been better or worse. Or when we contrast the problems we have now with those we had before, instead of thinking of permanent solutions we should think of permanent problems in the sense that one problem replaces another. Then we might ask whether today's answers are more moral or more effective than the solutions that they might replace. Are today's inflated medical costs preferable to yesterday's restricted access to medical care? The capacity of policies to generate more interesting successors, and our ability to learn from them what we ought to prefer, may be their most important quality.

I would like progress to return to public policy. I would especially like the people of this country to perceive correctly that their government is performing well and is worthy of their continued support. The question is how to make these fine-sounding phrases seem more than mere platitudes.

Returning to the criteria for considering progress, the problem is to make existing knowledge more adequate for proposed public policy. The objectives sought and the intellectual resources available to achieve them should be brought into greater consonance. Whereas incentives inside government favor error protection, they should be altered in favor of correction. Selection should overtake size as the prevailing principle in government. Government, if I am permitted a little rhetorical license, should look less like a dinosaur and more like a dolphin.

Nothing is good for everything. No nostrums will fix warts, backaches, and blisters. No magic elixir will cure all that ails us. But I believe that constitutional expenditure limitation will help reintroduce progress into public policy. By slowing down the rate of increase in spending by the federal government, the amendment will help policymakers improve their competence in relation to their problems. By reducing the proliferation of programs (because old ones will not be able to expand indefinitely and sizeable new programs will have to displace older ones) the knowledge required to run programs will also be reduced. By forcing competition, some selection will be inevitable. Consequently, as the size of government stops growing in relation to the size of the economy, a more varied society will respond more flexibly to new situations and public policy will be pinpointed to a smaller number of more specific problems. Government will be more selective internally and externally. Its relative size will decrease but its absolute capability will increase. Progress will be possible because government will no longer be known for its rigidity but for its resilience.

2

A Spending Limit As a Social Contract

PLACED IN WIDE perspective, the purpose of constitutional expenditure limitation is to increase cooperation in society and conflict in government. As things stand, the purveyors of public policy within government have every incentive to raise their spending income while reducing their internal differences. How? By increasing their total share of national income at the expense of the private sector. Why fight among their public selves if private persons will pay? They present a bill to Congress that, in effect, must be paid by higher taxes or bigger debt. Those who view government as an engine of income redistribution to increase equality do battle against those who stress leaving resources in the private sector so as to increase wealth. Thus conflict is transferred from government to society.

INCREASING COOPERATION IN SOCIETY AND CONFLICT IN GOVERNMENT

Once a limit was enacted, however, the direction of incentives would be radically reversed, resulting in increasing cooperation in society and rising conflict in government.

Citizens in society would have a common interest whereas the sectors of policy—housing, welfare, environment, defense— would be plunged into conflict. This change in perceived interest would be divided over the relative shares of each sector within a firmly fixed limit. Organizations interested in income redistribution favoring poor people would come to understand the fatal fact: the greater the increase in real national product the more there would be for government to spend on these purposes. Instead of acting as if it did not matter where the money came from, they would have to consider how they might contribute to enhanced productivity. Management and labor, majorities and minorities, would have to consider common objectives, how to urge more out of one another rather than how to take more.

So far it seems one-sided: the private economy and its supporters have always stood to gain from productivity. What will they give as well as get?—acceptance of welfare programs within the specified size of the public sector. Social welfare programs are objected to not because they improve the living conditions of the economically deprived, but because they engender fear that the public sector will grow and grow and grow until it swallows up the private sector, irreversibly altering the way of life in this country. The feeling that, as presently constituted, there is no end to it, is responsible for the reluctance to accept governmental assistance to the needy as a permanent (and desirable) part of American life. Given a constitutional guarantee that this cannot happen, the private sector can either leave the public to its own devices or can join in a common endeavor to improve the efficacy with which it delivers support to universally accepted public services.

Public involvement with private enterprise would take on a decidedly different character. "Produce more to distribute more" would be the slogan. Criticism of corporations would not be based on alleged obstruction of public purposes but on failure to further private productivity. Industry would be instructed to perform its tasks better rather than be lectured as lacking in social conscience or lagging in assuming social services. Governmental regulations that impose financial burdens would not be viewed as desirable in and of themselves, as if they were free, but would be balanced against the loss to the economy on which the size of social services depend.

Expenditure limitation would improve popular penetration of the public sector. In an era of big government, the administrative apparatus and the money it manages have not only grown larger but more opaque. Who can claim to see inside the Department of Defense or of Health and Welfare? These programs reach into every corner of the nation, buttressed by field offices, supplemented by state services, augmented by matching funds. The larger and the more numerous these programs become, extending literally from soup (school lunches) to nuts (price supports for peanuts), the more varied and indirect their consequences, the less laymen can know about them and the poorer the predictions of so-called experts. Yet the motivation to recognize and correct errors is missing. Knowledge of consequences is difficult to detect, because there are so many programs with such varied effects. Comparing results with intentions is both depressing (because they are so far apart) and destructive (because the maintenance of the organization and its clientele benefits would be threatened).

Look at it the other way round: if we are in favor of forestry or wish to mandate missiles, we want the agencies in charge to last, to survive small traumas, not to go into shock the first time something goes wrong. So we build organizational structures to survive. Thus it turns out that while small errors are difficult to detect but easy to correct, the large errors that are easy to spot are hard to change because so much money and so many people are implicated in their chain of consequences. Consequently, evaluation is mostly pro forma, informing the external world that the agency is all right rather than reforming its internal operations.

If paid professionals have difficulty, how will we-the-people ever find out what is going on inside public agencies? What is worse, how will the agencies? Ordinarily, they pay as little attention to each other as possible. Where a common concern is evident, they form interagency committees to share the blame (each initial "signing off" being a hostage against retribution) or the spoils; after all, their common conclusion is bound to be that more should be spent. Since they cannot predict the consequences of their activities and since they are unwilling to share their uncertainty (and hence their power), agencies adopt a cybernetic solution. They tacitly agree to cope with the consequences caused by other agencies just as the others agree to cope with theirs. The cost of coordination is reduced to a minimum.

What about the center (the President, the Office of Management and Budget, the Council of Economic Advisers, and the Treasury)? The center becomes another sector, specialized to macro-economic management. In return for deference on adjusting the economy, it agrees (again, tacitly) not to interfere in agency operations, which, in any case, are too many and too misunderstood to be dealt with in detail. This is how, as government grows more centralized in the sense that there are super-departments, the center disappears.[1] Neither the agencies nor their ostensible central controllers are engaged in evaluation leading to action.

How, in this context, might agencies be encouraged to monitor their own activities, as well as other related programs, making adjustments in the results achieved and the resources used? The usual method is to command that this be done. Almost all agencies are required to evaluate. Alas, nothing really requires them to do this well. Instead, the space devoted to evaluation looms so large, its sheer size becomes an obstacle to taking any single one seriously. Merely monitoring each evaluation would become a formidable task in itself. So, as I said, evaluation becomes an advertisement—I'm all right, Jack!, examined, evaluated, 99 and 44/100 percent pure, the Ivory Soap of analysis—instead of an action-oriented activity.

The alternative to central command is introducing incentives to guide interaction. How might not only doing but using evaluation be made in the interest of agencies? What would be in it for them? Back we go to making government competitive by limiting resources so as to increase internal conflict.

Before too long, when expenditure limitation takes hold, for every major addition to federal expenditure there will have to be an equivalent subtraction. The doctrine of opportunity costs, which states that the value of an act is measured in terms of opportunities foregone, will be alive and well in government. The consequences for agencies and the supporters of their programs will be profound. For the first time in modern history, they will know that more for one means less for the other.

The incentive to improve internal efficiency will be immense. Knowing that they are unlikely to get more and may well get less (depending on the state of the economy and disposition of the policy), agencies will try to get the most out of what they have. Efficiency will no longer be a secondary consideration, to be satisfied if nothing else is pressing, or be no consideration at all if evidence that they can do with less would reduce their future income: efficiency will be the primary path of the steady state in which they find themselves.

Two things will be happening at once: each agency will be figuring out how to defend what it has and how to steal a march on the others in getting new programs approved. Agencies will not be able to argue (as through time immemorial) merely that their proposal in and of itself is desirable (for there are few programs utterly without merit or benefit for someone) to expect that it might merit a higher priority than others currently being considered. They will need to demonstrate defects in other agency programs. Naturally, these other agencies will defend themselves. Instead of Congress and interested public officials having to ferret out weaknesses in agency programs, they themselves will accomplish that. Competition will improve information. In addition to outsiders demanding that agencies evaluate their own activities, insiders will insist that they do so as well. The opaque agency will become transparent.

Does this idyllic picture have no potential flaws, so that, like Dorian Gray, its accumulation of evil eventually will reveal the corruption underneath the smooth surface? Might not agencies, for instance, be embattled and therefore emboldened to mobilize their clientele in something like Hobbes's "War of All Against All?" Might there not, in a word, be more politics in spending rather than less? Of course. Part of the point of expenditure limitation is to make politics richer and more revealing for citizens in society. Promises of "pie in the sky by and by," as the old labor ditty has it, would be countered by vigorous and informed opposition from the agency personnel closest to the proposed program, who would be most disadvantaged by its expenditures. If political interaction produces desirable outcomes, it is not the amount of activity but the quality that counts.

LESS INFLATION, LOWER TAXES, BETTER BUDGETING, SMALLER SPENDING

Among the worst things that can be said about a policy or process, virtually an operational definition of bad government, is that it protects the governors against the consequences of their own actions. The epitome of this political obscenity, practiced, alas, among American congressmen as well as among British higher civil servants, is the protecting of their pensions against inflation. Even worse for the country, because inflation pushes people into higher tax brackets, is that government as a whole gains more in income than it loses in purchasing power during periods of prolonged inflation; tax income increases roughly one-and-a-half times for every increase in nominal income. This incentive to inflate is the kind of perverse effect of the existing political process that the expenditure limitation amendment is designed to counter.

It is commonly believed that government tries to slow

inflation because it is bad for the country. As the song says, "It ain't necessarily so." Around the world, inflation is fast becoming the main instrument of policy. Weak governments, unable to fulfill their promises and unwilling to keep from promising, use inflation to reduce the effective size of their national debt (which can then be paid back in cheaper dollars, pounds, or pesos), to redistribute income, or to reduce the real rewards of wage increases demanded under duress by unions. Though everyone in government by no means benefits, since the cost of certain services may rise faster than inflation, the administration in power has more money to give away without having to undergo the opprobrium of increasing taxes.

The amendment contains two mechanisms for inhibiting inflation—negative and positive. Since governmental income does not grow with inflation, there is no incentive to increase inflation. And if it is correct that the cost of services rises faster than inflation, inflation unaccompanied by even larger spending increases reduces the government's purchasing power. To strengthen its resolve, government will also lose spending power between the time the Executive Branch budget is introduced and the following fiscal year in which it is acted upon, for inflated prices will not be reflected in the earlier increase to national product on which the budget is based. Neither inflation during the budget year or afterward should pay off. I presume government would rather not incur this penalty. Other than the common sense of lowering expenditure during inflationary periods, I do not presume to offer advice on curbing inflation. Large sacrifices in employment or production should not be undertaken for small gains against inflation. But in large scale and on a continuing basis, I do believe inflation is a bad thing. Instead of exhortation against inflation, I rely on the brand of country wisdom which presumes that you are more likely to find something if you have reason to look for it.

The long amendment contains a more powerful disincentive. Should inflation rise about 3 percent, every additional

4 percent increase reduces permissible spending by 1 percent. The disadvantages of this approach are that the amendment becomes overly technical, and that sudden drops in spending may be destabilizing, especially if inflation depends mostly on factors outside the spending process. The advantage is that government must try harder—much harder—to curb inflation.

The difference between "nominal," current dollar, and real (keeping price changes constant) GNP must be kept in mind. The thrust of expenditure limitation is to relate the share of federal spending to the size of the economy. The limitation on outlays, therefore, is on nominal spending in proportion to the rise in nominal GNP. Thus allowable spending may be thought of as the increase in prices plus the increase in productivity. Since governmental purchases of goods and services as well as income transfers decline with price increases, the real increase in spending is confined to the rise in productivity. Should there be a period of steep price increases, government spending would rise in proportion. It might then seem that there had also been an equivalent increase in real government spending, but that would result from confusing nominal with real dollars. The provision in the long amendment penalizing inflation would drive down real spending in constant dollars, but nominal expenditure would continue to go up.

Though the amendment says nothing about taxation, except that revenues can only be used for outlays and for reducing the national debt, it must lead to tax reduction. Under a progressive income tax, each unit increase in income leads to a unit-and-a-half increase in revenue as people are pushed into higher brackets. Consequently, with expenditures limited to the increase in national income, the same tax rates as in the past will produce correspondingly more income. Unless the national debt is to be retired instead, revenue (and hence tax rates) will have to decline. Though a spending limitation does not necessarily change the composition of taxes—any form or method of taxation, however pro-

gressive or regressive, may be used—it will undoubtedly
reduce the total amount paid compared to what it otherwise
would have been.

It is hard to say no to tax reduction, but the question must
be raised of the equity, and therefore the legitimacy, of the
resulting tax structure. Would lower levels of taxation enhance or hinder tax reform? Would low rates close loopholes, as those who should pay do pay, or enhance equity, so
that those who have more pay more, or reduce the hidden
subsidies inherent in tax preferences? I believe they would.
The search for loopholes is propelled by the desire to escape
from high rates. When the government holds more of your
money than you do, it is only natural (though not necessarily
desirable) to devote as much attention to paying less as to
producing more. The lower the tax rates, however, the less
the incentive to go out of one's way (seek a tax shelter, charge
off a dinner, pursue a tax loss) to increase one's income.
With top rates reduced, say, from 70 to 30 percent, it would
be easier to outlaw exceptions and to increase the progres-
sivity of the rates.

Budgetary reform would also be enhanced by expenditure
limitation. Practically every year the principle of inclusive-
ness—all expenditures should be in the budget and compete
on the same basis—is subject to repeated violation. The term
"tax expenditure" has been coined to refer to leaving sums
that would otherwise be paid to government in the hands of
taxpayers so as to serve a public purpose, such as subsidizing
mortgage payments or state and local bond issues. These subsidies could just as well be made direct expenditures, subject
to the disciplines of the appropriations process. The same is
true of spending by governmentally sponsored corporations
and by rapidly growing loan guarantees. Even the bulk of
ordinary expenditure never passes through the appropriations process, because it is done by direct drafts on the Treasury (called by opponents "back-door" spending) in the
form of entitlements. On the grounds that "misery loves
company," one program's escape from the appropriation

process will, under the amendment, become another's deprivation. For as resources are diverted from private productivity to the public sector, they reduce the growth on which spending depends, thus increasing the incentive for those in the budget to get rid of those who profit at their expense by being allowed to stay out of it.

There are good reasons to believe, in conclusion, that the amendment would result in smaller spending, lower taxes, and less inflation. A bonus of tax and budget reform is thrown in as an added attraction. If all this is so desirable, why doesn't every man, woman, and child in the country line up to accomplish it? If this is so easy, how come our politicians and political processes do not rush to ratify it to the hosannas of the people? Good questions deserve good answers.

This proposed social contract dividing resources between the private and public sectors will also exert profound effects on the economy—growth, employment, and inflation; on the polity—the distribution of benefits; and on the society—relationships among groups who will have decided that they should not look to the public sector as the dominant force in their private lives. Understanding who wins and who loses, as the title of the sixth lecture suggests, is essential to determining whether the amendment is desirable. Yet, if everyone agrees on whom the amendment indulges and whom it deprives, it will be defeated as class legislation. If there is reason to believe that fundamental interests in social welfare and national defense will be underprotected, the amendment will languish for lack of support. If many interests are overprotected, the amendment will be dismissed as unfair. Though there must be some uncertainty over outcomes, I shall argue it is not so substantial as to threaten basic American values.

There are two main criticisms of the amendment—it will not work as intended and it will wreak havoc if it does. Spending is supposed to be inexorable. Like a mighty torrent fed by raging tributaries, spending, if blocked one way, will spill over another. Once in the grip of a strict ceiling, it might be admitted, agencies should behave as advertised; it is their efforts to circumvent this ceiling that will create difficulties. By placing the limit not on appropriations or obligations but on outlays, defined as all payments made, the amendment should effectively prevent use of government corporations or other "off-budget" devices. But regulations that impose costs on private persons, subsidized credit, and tax expenditures that leave money in private hands before it gets to government, cannot be so conveniently countered. The fifth lecture on "end runs" will discuss these at length.

Expenditure limitation is also deemed defective because it proposes to place the political process under constraint. Evidently, people who propose a constitutional amendment must find politics as usual unsatisfactory. Evidently, they believe that the ordinary legislative process will not accomplish these purposes. Do they distrust democracy? As presently constituted, they must. Is there reason, then, to believe a constitutional reform would improve the everyday operation of politics? Even if it would, might not the same result be reached by perfecting politics: What is stopping Americans from cutting spending, program by program, one at a time, like any intelligent people would? Why tamper with the Constitution, thereby inflaming passions and possibly introducing rigidities that people of good sense would just as soon see disappear? These questions are addressed in the fourth lecture on why constitutional self-limitation is necessary for self-control over spending. The defect I see in the political process is of a classical kind: people object to the collective consequences of choices they have taken one at a time. "The Pogo Principle," the third lecture, argues that we-the-people can undo constitutionally what we do not like about our own behavior.

Disappointment, if not distrust of political processes, is a major motivation behind many constitutional amendments. The Bill of Rights and the anti-third term provision are but two examples. Expenditure limitation is no exception. In what respects, and in which ways, we may ask, are present political processes deemed defective? And why, if these defects are basic, fundamental rather than peripheral, so a constitutional amendment is advocated to set them right, have they not manifested themselves so severely until our times? What has happened to the traditional restraints—reluctance to raise taxes, fear of retribution at the polls, belief in a balanced budget, the economizing orientation of the Appropriations Committees, ceilings on the national debt, and all the rest—that used to keep spending down? Something must have happened to the Treasury along the way or spending limits would not be an issue. (Bringing up limits on the national debt, changed upward automatically by a Congress unwilling to let government grind to a halt, by the way, reminds us of why a constitutional amendment, with its requirement for extraordinary majorities, might be preferable to ordinary legislation.)[2] Only history (the second lecture) can tell us why the protections of the past have become the profligacy of the present.

3

Constitution Making as Error Correction: Why Defects in the Structure of Spending Were Not Evident Earlier in American History

EVERY CONSTITUTION IS written against the last usurper. Ours is no exception. The Constitution of the United States of America came into being in order to form a union more perfect than that established by the Articles of Confederation. As the call for the Constitutional Convention stated:

That there are important defects in the system of the Fœderal Government is acknowledged by the Acts of all those States, which have concurred in the present Meeting; That the defects, upon a closer examination, may be found greater and more numerous, than even these acts imply, is at least so far probable, from the embarrassments which characterise the present State of our national affairs, foreign and domestic, as may reasonably be supposed to merit a deliberate and candid discussion.[1]

This confederate form of government, which entrenched state sovereignty, was too strong to be useful to citizens who sought change from within and too weak to preserve domes-

[44]

tic tranquility. State governments, in the framers' view, allowed cheap money to invade the interests of creditors, but their combined influence was more than sufficient to prevent the confederation from counteracting the consequences. What would prevent government under the new constitution from merely transferring the same error to the federal government, whose overriding power would enable it to commit as well as to prevent evil? The founding fathers cited two deterrents: the structure of government and the extent of the country. When opponents of a national government (as well as earlier theorists) claimed that republics were viable only when they were small, this argument was turned against them.

In what he called the theory of a "compound republic," James Madison expressed his hope and belief that the large geographic size of the country, as well as the variety of its peoples, would retard the formation of factions (which we would call pressure groups) acting adversely to the interests of others. It would, he thought, be too difficult for factions to organize, confer, and act unless they were numerous and until they had secured widespread agreement. Organized interests would be few in number but large in size, reflecting in the very process of formation a general interest likely to be in accord with a shared view of justice. In Madison's words,

The other point of difference is, the greater number of citizens and extent of territory... and it is this circumstance principally which renders factious combinations less to be dreaded in the former than in the latter. The smaller the society, the fewer probably will be the distinct parties and interests composing it; the fewer the distinct parties and interests, the more frequently will a majority be found of the same party; and the smaller the number of individuals composing a majority, and the smaller the compass within which they are placed, the more easily will they concert and execute their plans of oppression. Extend the sphere, and you take in a greater variety of parties and interests; you make it less probable that a majority of the whole will have a common motive to invade the rights of other citizens; or if such a common motive exists, it will be more difficult for all who feel it to discover their own strength, and to act in unison with each other. Besides other impediments, it may be remarked that, where there is a consciousness of unjust or dishonorable purposes, communication is always checked by distrust in proportion to the number whose concurrence is necessary.[2]

Modern technology has undermined these Madisonian premises. It is far easier and cheaper for people to get together than ever he could have imagined. Groups aiming at government are today more numerous and specialized and this process of differentiation shows no signs of stopping. All around the western world, articulation of interest increases with size of population, frequency of interaction, and growth of government, which makes it worthwhile to get together.[3]

If modern means of communication were unanticipated, the reversal of political causality, comparable perhaps to redirecting magnetism, was not even dreamed about. Factions exerted force on government, not the other way round. Government might resist but it could on no account create faction. In Madison's words, faction might be sown in the nature of man but not at the behest of government. Yet, with big government, this is exactly what happens. The more government does for or to industry and individuals (which hardly matters) the more it must continue to do. Instead of industry instigating action by government, for instance, we now know that often government acts and industry reacts. Industry's organized response is to an interest that government has, by its behavior, newly created. So, too, do other levels of government—state, counties, cities, special districts —organize to expand grants-in-aid after they have observed incentives created by the federal government.[4] Indeed, government now pays citizens to organize, lawyers to sue, and politicians to run for office. Soon enough, if current trends continue, government will become self-contained, generating (apparently spontaneously) the forces to which it responds.

The missing actor, like the dog that didn't bark, is as important as the whole cast of characters. I refer, of course, to the political party, whose emergence as an integrating device with a concern for its own future served (with the notable exception of slavery) to integrate demands. Extremism was eliminated or tamed or co-opted. The good name of the party could not be maintained by identification with policies whose future consequences brought it into disrepute. Too much for a single interest would mean too little for another. As their nominating and employment functions eroded under the onslaught of primaries and civil service, however, parties of integration grew progressively weaker. (Where, oh where, were the Republican Party leaders insisting that former President Nixon come clean over Watergate? And where are Democrats reconciling minorities and labor, or the poor and pregnant, to the anti-abortionites?) It is not single issue interest groups that are worrisome, but the lack of strong political institutions simultaneously to moderate their demands and to meliorate their conditions.

Even if factions had been able to form, in the constitutional scheme of things they should not have been able to fulfill their objectives; the framers thought that interrelationship among institutions and the differentiation of the electorate would see to that. "Ambition would counteract ambition" as the holders of office, elected for staggered terms from different constituencies, would compete and therefore contain each other. Nowadays the separation of powers, checks and balances, and federalism have become not only tried and true but trite. So we no longer ask whether they operate as they once used to do. We should.

SECTORS AS SPENDERS

In the past, the mechanisms of integration were out in society bringing people together so they could be served by government. The mechanisms were not internal, unifying the government against the people it was supposed to serve. Institutions were separated so that each would have an incentive, not only to perform its prescribed duties, but to keep the others in close confines. Congress could pass laws over the

President's veto. He held the executive power. They could cooperate or they could conflict, but they could not conspire. Since congressmen were supposed to come from different constituencies (senators elected by state legislature, congressmen by the electorate) as was the President (chosen by elites indirectly through an Electoral College conceived as an independent, deliberative body), unity of views was neither expected nor necessary. Where 'the good' was evident to broad publics, it would be done. Where it was not agreed upon, it need not be observed. Stalemate was not necessarily desirable but it was acceptable.

Now all this has changed; integration of society through parties outside government has been replaced by integration of what Hugh Heclo has called *issue networks* inside government.[5] These networks are composed of people who work full time in sectors of policy, whether they be bureaucrats, congressmen, congressional staff, state and local officials, or consultants. What they give in common is full-time attention to issues in their sector. The more important the network becomes and the larger it grows, the higher their status and the broader their opportunities. Whatever their differences, they are the ones who have the understanding to participate; whatever goes wrong, they will be the ones to create remedies; whatever changes are made, they will be the innovators.

Instead of a separation of powers, therefore, there exists a unification of interests based on a functional division of labor among sectors of policy. Bargaining takes place within sectors, from health to transportation to agriculture, but not among them. The center (the Presidency, the Federal Reserve Board, the Treasury) becomes another sector superintending macro-economic management of the economy. Coordination is not achieved by central command nor is it accomplished by accommodation among external interests mediated through political parties. Coordination is cybernetic; each sector acts independently, feeling free to create consequences for others (as welfare policy affects criminal justice) so long as it accepts the effects of other sector policies on its own programs. The size of government and the insignificance of parties have combined to produce this result.

This line of sectors, each with a hand on the shoulder of the one nearest to it, could be described as engaging in a game of reverse musical chairs—when the singing stops there are extra chairs to fill. Their golden rule is that each may do unto the other as the other does unto it so long as there is more for both. The litany is well known, especially at appropriations hearings: doing well deserves more and doing badly deserves mountains of money because these unfortunate conditions must be alleviated. What must never happen to shatter the chain is for one sector to take resources from another. To beggar thy neighbor is verboten. The rule of "fair-shares" is characteristic, dividing equally among agencies any increases over the prior year and any decreases from requests.[6] Extraordinary programs with special appeal may go up so long as others do not go down. Thus defense will not decrease but may be kept constant while welfare grows. How are these happy accommodations possible? Because the public sector has been able to solve its internal problems both by absorbing the growth and by decreasing the share of the private sector.

Summing up the system of incentives in central government spending, addition is easier than subtraction. Whenever there is a crunch, administrative agencies will add on the costs of their programmatic proposals; they will not, unless compelled, subtract one from the other. (They do not, to be sure, ask for all they would like, only for more than they already have; their proposals are cut, only their spending is not.) Subtraction suggests competition in which there have to be losers; addition is about cooperation in which (within government) there are only winners. When the economy produces sufficient surplus, spending grows painlessly; when there is not quite enough to go around, spending grows noiselessly as inflation increases effective taxation, or as tax expenditures and loan guarantees substitute for amounts that would otherwise appear in the budget. The budget grows.

A downward dip now and again does not slow its inexorable progress. Why does this imperfection in political processes occur?

The subdivision of society into sectors of public policy has profound implications for the control of public expenditures. Were the cause in the bureaucracy, it could be controlled. Were the fault found in Congress, it could be changed. Were the Presidency propelled by spending, it could be stopped. If internal controls were inadequate, external controls could be applied through the normal operation of checks by separate powers. However, if separate institutions no longer share powers, as Richard Neustadt wrote, but separate sectors share institutions, how and by whom is control exercised?

Not by the traditional central control organs, for the center has been sectoralized; everywhere, ministers of finance or secretaries of the treasury and chairs of the Council of Economic Advisors are primarily interested in the economy, not in spending. And the sectors themselves are spenders. Old-fashioned politics dealing with a single sector at a time will not do, because more will be left for the remainder rather than less for all.

Whatever is done to limit spending, therefore, must affect the sectors all at once. Competition must be restored, not among institutions, which are conduits colonized by sectors, but among the sectors so that the public cannot gain at the expense of the private, and so that single sectors can gain only from their share of the increase in the private. Instead of the public sector alone playing a positive sum game, where all agencies gain by invading the private sector, or a zero-sum game, in which private losses are public gains, there should be a joint game for all society in which the public and the private sectors share the same fate.

WHERE IS THE INSTITUTIONAL BREAKDOWN?

Before we can produce this positive result, however, we must ask ourselves how and why the invasion of the private by the public sector has been allowed to begin and has been able to succeed? Perhaps the answer is simpler than anyone suggests: Working their will through democratic procedures, people are doing and getting what they want. Otherwise, as Brian Barry states so well, it is "important to know if the forces of electoral competition can be expected to operate in some systematic way to give people what they don't want, or more specifically to give them something that would be defeated by some alternative in a straight vote. For this would suggest that there is some kind of internal flaw to democracy."[7] Barry is inclined to believe there is no such flaw, or if there is, that it is not of the kind leading to undesired, high expenditures. Those who hold opposing views are also troubled by the thought that the political process is right and they are wrong. Their perplexity is worth pursuing. According to James Buchanan and Richard Wagner,

> The question we must ask, and answer, is: Why do citizens support politicians whose decisions yield the results we have described? If citizens are fully informed about the ultimate consequences of alternative policy choices, and if they are rational, they should reject political office seekers or officeholders who are fiscally irresponsible. They should not lend indirect approval to inflation-inducing monetary and fiscal policy; they should not sanction cumulatively increasing budget deficits and the public-sector bias which results. Yet we seem to observe precisely such outcomes.[8]

> There is a paradox of sorts here. A regime of continuous and mounting deficits, with subsequent inflation, along with a bloated public sector, can scarcely be judged beneficial to anyone. Yet why does the working or ordinary democratic process seemingly produce such a regime? Where is the institutional breakdown?[9]

Let us seek enlightenment on the historical side of the subject: What was it that, with the exception of war, led the nation, throughout its history, to produce relatively small budgets with expenditures and revenues within hailing distance?

To say that public officials once believed in the doctrine of the desirability of a balanced budget may seem like answering one question with another. What we want to know is why this doctrine was believed and acted upon and then abandoned. All these questions may be answered by focusing on the doctrine that replaced it, the neo-Keynesian idea of balance termed the *full-employment surplus,* a doctrine under which there would almost always be a deficit. The balanced budget was everything the full-employment surplus was not.

From the earliest beginnings of the American Republic until 1960, budgets were almost always in balance. Following the rule of a balanced budget was an effective mechanism for keeping expenditures down. The dislike of raising taxes exerted restraint on expenditure. Deficits were tolerated during emergencies—wartime and recession. But politicians expected retribution if they didn't obey the rule. The value of a balanced budget has been eroded on one side by technical developments: the replacement of the old cash budget with an administrative budget (including a wide variety of transactions, all sorts of trust funds and transfer payments) has made the meaning of a particular level of deficit problematical. The larger the size of the total budget, the more important small differences in estimates (5 percent of $600 billion compared to 5 percent of $100 billion) become, so that the last $10 to $30 or more billion may be pure guesswork. It is the erosion of the balanced budget ideology and its replacement by the ideology of balancing the economy that has made the deepest impression.

The attraction of Keynesianism itself is easy to understand. It involves just two variables—spend more when the economy is too slow, spend less when it is going too fast—that politicians on the run believe they can understand and, what is more important, can manipulate. The full-employment surplus is even more attractive. Don't just balance the budget, dummy, balance the economy! Why worry about a purely technical balance when you are leaving resources and people underutilized. Spend to save. Old-fashioned ideas about the government being like the family, which must not spend more than it takes in, or inflation being connected to using debt financing and money creation to cover deficits, went by the boards. Eventually, higher levels of economic activity would generate greater revenues to bring the budget into balance. (The Kemp-Roth Bill, based on economist Arthur Laffer's work, promised to do the same thing by drastic reductions in taxes, which, in theory, would eventually generate productivity to increase revenues.) Today, the arrival of "stagflation," that is, simultaneous unemployment and inflation, threatens to undermine the entire Keynesian edifice. For us, however, the important thing is that once balancing the economy becomes the norm, expenditure can undergo enormous expansion with the blessing of economic doctrine. The full-employment surplus was a license (almost a commandment) to spend.

During the time of Presidents Truman and Eisenhower, the operative fiscal rule concerned a balanced budget. At the risk of some simplification, Truman would essentially take existing domestic spending, add on something he would like or could get through Congress, add or subtract a little according to the employment situation, and devote what was left (within a balanced budget) to defense. At the same time, of course, he kept in mind what he considered minimum essentials necessary to support national defense. Eisenhower also worked within a balanced budget framework, except that he was rather more concerned with inflation and with the division of shares between the private economy and the public sector. Using his own considerable judgment, backed up by National Security Council staff papers, he fixed the defense budget after the Korean conflict at around $35 billion dollars, so that there would be room for tax reduction within a nearly balanced budget. Because both Truman and Eisenhower believed in balanced budgets, and because Truman could not get expensive spending programs passed and Eisenhower did not want them, and because both were willing to impose spending ceilings on defense, they were able to keep revenues and expenditures roughly in line.[10]

Kennedy and Johnson changed all that. The shibboleth of the balanced budget held little attraction for them. Kennedy was mainly interested in economic growth to create the larger society capable of fulfilling his ambitious plans in space and on earth. Kennedy's transitional "new economics," under which discretionary deficits were possible and a strong tax reduction stimulus was desirable, opened more room for both defense and domestic spending. Under Johnson, the military budget went up to reflect spending on the war in Vietnam and domestic expenditures rose because of commitment to the war on poverty. The remnants of the balanced budget ideology went down with Johnson's "guns and butter" approach.

Among the many surprises of the Nixon administration was the Keynesian concept of full-employment surplus, where a deficit was permissible so long as its size did not exceed the level of revenues that would have been achieved had the nation been at full employment. That a conservative (if opportunistic) administration found this doctrine appealing suggests that it has a great deal to offer politicians. Because the concept of full employment surplus is not overly precise, the question of an appropriate level of spending depends on judgmental variables—on tax estimates, on the velocity with which money moves through the economy, on the impact of deficits spent in different ways, and on more factors than can be recounted here. Best of all, spending, however high according to old-fashioned notions, is never larger than it should be.

GETTING WHAT YOU WANT DOES NOT NECESSARILY MEAN YOU WANT WHAT YOU GET

Again, it appears that we have answered one question with another: why does this scenario for super spending find favor now when it didn't then? Another hypothesis, at the risk of overstating the obvious, is that people have the money now and they didn't then. Resource production, the increase in real national income together with a quantum leap forward in resource extraction, and taxes of all kinds, collected with consummate skill, have expanded national horizons. In few words, spending has gone up along with everything else. Most money is collected from income taxes. The passage of the Sixteenth Amendment authorizing this tax is a major constitutional development. Yet it can hardly be said that this was put over on the people. Presumably, we got what we wanted and have been getting it ever since.

The same can be said of judicial interpretations of the commerce clause, the general welfare clause, the necessary and proper clause, and the Tenth Amendment reserving to the states all powers not granted to the federal government. Whether or not the Supreme Court follows the election returns, it is difficult to argue that it has expanded national powers in these areas which facilitate federal expenditures, all against the tide of public opinion. The court may lead opinion here or there, but it cannot be wholly at variance with it. Were that so, an angry President and Congress could appoint more sympathetic members or narrow its jurisdiction or otherwise control the Court.

Two truths stand out; things have changed to encourage larger expenditures; and it is not clear that this has been done against the will of the people. But we-the-people do not have to want what we have willed. The purpose of policy analysis is not to help us get what we once erroneously thought was desirable, but to perfect our preferences, to teach us what we ought to want. Having willed the means but not the end, we must now employ different and more efficacious means for the end we would have willed had we known what would happen. Nor should we try to turn back the clock. It is always a world we never made; we did not wish it to be entirely what it has become or we would not want to be changing it. The thing is to go from where we are to a better place, not to spend our time wishing we were not here at all. The recognition that we face a common problem is helpful in thinking about a common answer—a constraint on all our behavior, as citizen and as officials, so that there is an appropriate balance between our public proclivities and private activities. As someone once said, "America is promises." This time we promise not to promise so much.

Whether we are talking about things we have done to ourselves or that organized interests have done to us (I urge accepting personal responsibility) the results are the same—continuously higher expenditures. Where others organize against us, they take our tax money because they care and know more; their personal benefits are greater than our individual costs. By summing all these expenditures, so they stand out, and by forcing them to fit within a fixed limit, so competition reveals their weakness, majorities as well as minorities are given a chance to have their say. Where we do ourselves in—the Pogo Theory of the next lecture—the common criticism is that if we had known how much it would cost, we might not have done it. Inserting a cost constraint would cure that ill.

When I was writing *The Politics of the Budgetary Process* in the early 1960s, by way of recapitulation, the federal budgetary process appeared to be a marvelous example of coordination without a coordinator. Without a central direction, expenditures were close to revenues, evidencing a slow and gentle rise that could be accelerated or reversed in incremental steps without too much trouble. What was remarkable, it seemed to me, was that the games the participants played fell within well-defined boundaries, compensating for their crudities and inefficiencies by keeping within the rules.

In retrospect, it all seems idyllic. Suddenly the mechanisms of coordination—belief in a balanced budget, national political parties, Congressional cohesion, a slow rate of development permitting programs and their finances to grow together—all disappeared or were weakened. Within a generation expenditures all went up, and no one knew how to make the old folk adage—whatever goes up has to come down—a reality.

Disciplines that were once unnecessary because big government had not yet arrived must now be invented. Expenditure limitation via constitutional amendment is a formal replacement for what once was an informal understanding. Why can't we recapture the old time religion (at least in regard to expenditure)? Why, if we acknowledge having done wrong, don't we trust ourselves to do right? Having said that we are our own problem, I must explain why we might want to rescue ourselves by imposing limits on our own behavior.

4

The Pogo Principle

MAY I SAY emphatically that I do not subscribe to theories of bureaucratic conspiracy or manipulation by politicians to explain the growth of public expenditure. "What," asks Brian Barry, "could anyone hope for from a system characterized by a collection of rogues competing for the favors of a larger collection of dupes?"[1] I wish to puncture the Parkinsonian proposition that bureaucrats expand their programs indefinitely by hoodwinking the population. Were these programs not deeply desired by strong social elements, they would not prosper. As Frank Levy told me, it is not the conspiracy theory but the Pogo Theory that is applicable: *We have seen the enemy and they are us.*

A CRITIQUE OF CONSPIRACY THEORIES

The elegant theory of bureaucracy propounded by William Niskanen is intuitively appealing and aesthetically pleasing. "By what criteria," he asks, "are bureaucrats judged and rewarded?" The difference between the results they achieve and the resources their agencies consume are not factors. Bureaucrats can neither appropriate savings nor can their

[58]

agencies carry over funds. Their opportunities for promotion, for salary, and for influence increase with size irrespective of success. They will want more (much more) for their agencies and programs than citizens would prefer under similar circumstances.[2] So far so good. But why would citizens as voters elect governmental officials who would go along with this? If citizens think taxes are too high or expenditures too large, what stops them from using the ballot box to enforce these views?

I reject the conspiratorial views of the left (false consciousness) or of the right (fiscal illusion), not because they are wholly wrong, but because a partial truth is often worse than none at all. Baldly stated, the doctrine of false consciousness alleges that in capitalist countries the masses are indoctrinated to prefer policies contrary to their real interests by a biased transmission of culture, from schools to churches to the media of communication. No doubt all of us mistake our interests: no one can jump out of his skin and pretend to be born anew, untouched by human hands or immune from the presuppositions of his society. None of this, however, signifies that others have a true consciousness enabling them to know what is better for us than we do. In any event, in the current context, false consciousness would signify that expenditures are too low rather than too high, led by corporate propaganda to prefer private to public spending. As social workers would say, this is not the presenting problem.

Stripped of its surface of complex calculation, everyone can understand fiscal illusion, because no one understands ramifications of innumerable taxes and expenditures.[3] And citizens may systematically underestimate what they pay and what the government spends. That they pay a lot in sales, real estate, state, and federal income taxes, and all the rest is obvious to most people. Witness Proposition Thirteen. But at the federal level, the United States uses far fewer indirect taxes, which might escape notice, than do most western industrial nations. Undoubtedly, in view of the unfathomable billions involved, citizens also underestimate the costs of various programs. Since it would take only a few minutes for them to find out, however, I am not persuaded that this matters much. Illusions exist, no doubt, but I doubt that they result in the euphoric feeling of escape from taxation.

Life abounds with (some say it is composed of) illusions; given the complexity of the calculations, consciousness can hardly be correct all of the time. So what? So this is life. Nothing here explains a systematic unidirectional bias. As far as anyone can tell in regard to expenditure, our various incapacities cancel each other out. There would be more reason for concern if political processes operated so as to exclude certain interests altogether. When something is being taken away, for instance, existing interests may mobilize and countervailing power may be expected to produce reasonable results. Thus environmentalists would find it difficult to deprive people directly of employment. Should a new plant not be located near poor people for environmental reasons, however, the people affected might never know what they missed. Similarly, housing costs are driven up by harassment and litigation, as Bernard Frieden shows, with only minuscule ecological advantages, leaving the home buyer worse off without anyone realizing what has happened.[4] When the builder and the environmentalist sit alone at the table they may agree to produce one-tenth the housing at ten times the cost, but the little man who wasn't there suffers from higher-priced or more remote housing. The lesson to be learned is that any mechanism that makes people aware of losses and gains, so they can protect themselves, is better than one that allows them to be exploited in the name of public interest. If that sounds like expenditure limitation, so be it.

Both false consciousness and fiscal illusion serve the function of explaining to followers why a left- or right-wing movement fails. They are the doctrines of inveterate losers—"It can't be that the people are against us; it must be that they are misguided." These are not the people of whom Alexander Hamilton spoke ("Your people, sir, are a great beast!''). These are virtuous, benevolent, misguided people who, if they had the right information, would decide with full consciousness and without illusion to make the right (or is it left?) choice.

Other observers of sound mind and sane disposition consider the public sector to be underfinanced. In explaining "Why the Government Budget Is Too Small in a Democracy," Anthony Downs argues that a fully informed majority would want larger expenditure. This is so because voters (whom politicians try to please in party competition) are consistently misinformed; they perceive their tax burden more readily than the advantages of programs, many of which do not benefit them personally. This poor perception leads to the erroneous conclusion that government costs more than its programs are worth.[5] The difficulty with Downs is that the opposite assumption—benefits are palpable and appear to be free, because they are not paid for in cash, whereas taxes have to be paid anyway or are hidden in the price of commodities—appears equally plausible. Were Downs correct, it would be hard to explain why taxing and spending, spending and taxing, go up and up instead of down and down. Since total taxes and spending are widely perceived to be too high, not too low, an expenditure limit tied to economic growth would appear well aimed to restore the relationship between individual items and total expenditures, no matter why they have drifted apart.

Arguing that society is affluent but that public facilities are starved, John K. Galbraith insists that individuals are indoctrinated by advertising into artificial wants—into consumption for its own sake. Government, by contrast, is unable to advertise. Citizens would be better served, he asserts, if they would give more income to government for public purposes.[6] Aside from the fact that advertising is not always successful, and that people in countries without advertising appear to have remarkably similar preferences, the great question is why what Galbraith wants or what government does is superior to private preferences. Governmental advertising, in the form of public relations, actually is ubiquitous; Galbraith's complaint must really be that it is ineffective. Is he arguing that politics is superior to economics? Not quite. Is he saying that some wants are superior to others? No doubt. What, then, distinguishes his or my preferences from yours and theirs?

Another view, with which I also disagree in part, is Gordon Tulloch's theory that "the growth of the bureaucracy to a large extent is self-generating."[7] The trouble with bureaucrats is that they vote: the more of them there are, the more votes they have and the larger they grow. In support of this hypothesis, (un)certain evidence may be adduced. Civil servants on the average are about twice as likely to vote as other people. Governments at the state and local levels, where most civil servants are employed, are much more labor intensive than private industry, not only where they perform services, as Baumol's theory of increasing cost of service suggests,[8] but across the board. And the larger the size of government, the higher its proportion of administrative costs.[9] All this is tantalizing but far from conclusive. Bureaucrats are by no means a majority. If I should be correct in believing that, in their role as citizens, they don't like big government much more than do the rest of us, they wouldn't vote for expansion in general. They defend only their part of the public purse. Indeed, according to poll data, 48 percent of state employees in California said they would vote for Proposition Thirteen. The grand queries remain: Why don't the rest of us stop them or, even better, why don't their private selves stop their public selves?

DOING IT TO OURSELVES

By contrast, the Pogo Theory holds that we-the-people (including citizens, politicians, and civil servants) are doing this to ourselves. This is a cooperative game. We don't like it—

who said that people necessarily like what they do to themselves?—but we do do it. How? Why?

Not only the big, bad bureaucrats and their political protectors but, as the song says, "you and me babe" are at the root of our own problems. All of us are pure as the driven snow; it's just that we keep pushing expenditures up. Citizens like some of those programs. Indeed they do. Not all, of course, but enough to want to see them go up. Unfortunately, the only way to do that is to push everything up, partly because that is the price of support from other citizens (you provide the scratch for my program and I'll provide the scratch for yours), partly because that is the necessary exchange with politicians who support our programs and others, partly because there is usually no way to express a position on total spending aside from the items that make it up. Citizens want some spending more than others; they want their priorities to prevail; among these priorities is a preference for lower expenditure. Only the existence of the referendum route in California permits voters to say that real estate taxes are too high without simultaneously having to repudiate their political parties or their representatives in the state legislature, who they may still have preferred on other grounds. Public policy requires not only an aim but an avenue of redress.

Bureaucrats are no better. Just because they actively want more or passively can't resist does not mean they want the government to grow, at least not so fast. It's just that everybody is doing the same thing, or they can't get theirs without going along with those other programs. Like the citizenry (hell, they *are* the citizenry, at least a good part of it), bureaucrats bid up the cost of government without knowing they are doing so. As the hero used to say in those old-fashioned seduction scenes, when he was inexperienced and she was eager, "It's bigger than the both of us." How did we (not them but us), the people of the United States of America, get to be expenditure junkies? More to the point, how do we kick the habit?

ALPHONSE AND GASTON ON PUBLIC EXPENDITURE

Who would take the lead in reducing expenditures? Each sector of policy is concerned with its own internal development. More money makes it easier to settle internal quarrels. Those who believe more is better for their agency or their clientele come to this position naturally. Those who favor radical restructuring of programs soon discover that this is exceedingly difficult to do without sweetening the pie. All internal incentives work to raise expenditures. The price of policy change is program expansion.

The lessons of experience (as well as the lore of politicians) tells us that welfare policies can only be changed if their successors are larger (and emphatically costlier) than their predecessors. Are there, one wonders, apparently irreversible processes at work pushing up the prices of these programs? The large number of people benefitting from these programs must exert an influence on the increase in benefits. Perhaps their lobbyists also have reason to believe that the more people covered, the greater their influence, though this expansion also exacerbates the question of cost. In any event, the very fact that beneficiaries benefit personally and substantially, whereas other citizens are only tangentially involved, suggests the superiority of the interested over the uninformed in helping to determine governmental policy.

Viewing welfare from the perspective of popular preferences, it can be said that the people have approved the criteria according to which policies are created that vastly increase expenditures. Without bothering with a formal announcement, Americans have apparently agreed on three things: (1) no category of people, once covered, may be denied future benefits; (2) no level of benefits, once raised, may be reduced; and (3) given a choice between bringing benefits to all who qualify, even if some unqualified get in, or leaving out all the unqualified, even if some qualified don't make it, the former, accentuating the positive, is preferable. That is why there are headlines when people are underpaid but none when there are overpayments. Following these rules guarantees that every new program, if it is not just to do more of the same, must be larger than its predecessors. Otherwise, the most comprehensive coverage for the largest number of potential beneficiaries could not be guaranteed.[10] Yet excessive welfare costs are a common contemporary complaint.

Congressmen complain, too, but they don't do anything about it. Periodically Congress has been tightly organized under central leadership or under committee chairmen chosen in a seniority system giving weight to longevity. Appropriations positions have been occupied by people from safe districts who could afford to say no. Now, as everyone knows, the ability of individual legislators to express themselves has increased as their internal cohesion has decreased. As a consequence, appropriations have steadily risen and, where they would not, tunnels have been dug around them in the form of entitlements and tax expenditures, annual authorizations to put pressure on appropriations committees, varieties of backdoor "spending," subsidized credit, and all the rest. Congress has become fragmented; its members and their substantial staffs are as much a part of the sectors of policy as anyone else.

Of all those writing on these subjects, William Riker in his explanation of legislative expansion of the public sector comes closest, in my view, to the correct spirit. Riker says:

I think it is probably the case that, if everyone (or if all rulers in a society) agreed to do so, they could obtain the benefits of reducing the size of the public sector. But no such agreement occurs and our question is to explain why it does not. The explanation I offer is that rulers are trapped in a system of exchange of benefits that leads to disadvantageous . . . results. The system works in this way:

Step 1: Some legislator (or the leaders or some identifiable group with access to legislators) see an opportunity for gain for some of the legislator's constituents by the transfer of some activity from the private sector to the public sector. Usually such gain involves the transfer of a private cost to the public treasury. . . . Typically, of course, the beneficiaries of the transfer are relatively small groups of citizens and only a minority of legislators have constituents in the benefiting groups. Typically also there exist other groups and other minorities of legislators who see opportunities for private gain in other transfers from private to public sectors. The combination of several minorities of legislators acting to benefit constituents are enough to make a legislative majority and so together they can produce significant expansions of the public sector.

Step 2: Such a coalition would be socially harmless (though perhaps unfair).... But, of course, this successful coalition is only one of many. Entirely different coalitions, some overlapping, some not, obtain other kinds of transfers to the public sector: coalitions around public works, around military bases and contracting, around regulatory bodies and the favors they pass out to various small economic interests, et. Beyond economic interests there are ideological interests around which legislators can ally themselves to win support by satisfying deeply felt values of some constituents: racial, ethnic, linguistic, religious, moral, patriotic, etc.—all of which can be promoted by expansions of public sector activities. The consequence is that nearly every conceivable interest, economic and political, has some legislators promoting their own fortunes in future elections by promoting governmental service to that interest.

Step 3: Since each citizen with one or several interests served by these (usually minority) coalitions of legislators benefit as the coalitions succeed and since each legislator benefits in some degree from the gratitude thus generated in marginally important voters, nearly everyone benefits from successful actions to expand the public sector. Consequently, every legislator has a driving motive to form more or less ad hoc majority alliances of these minority coalitions in order to obtain some public benefits for every interest represented in the alliance. Were a legislator to refrain either from promoting some minority interests or from joining in larger alliances to obtain benefits, he (and his constituents) would merely suffer the costs of paying for the benefits for others while obtaining no benefits for themselves. Yet in the end the society has a greatly expanded public sector with very high costs and considerable inefficiencies. It seems very likely to me that these disadvantages are so great that nearly everybody is worse off than if the public sector expansion had never taken place. It might be supposed, therefore, that everybody would have a motive to agree to forego public sector benefits —and indeed they do. But an agreement for a grand coalition for abstinence seems well-nigh unenforceable. Everyone has a motive to desert the grand coalition in the hope of getting some public sector benefit before others do so.[11]

The only difference between us is one of emphasis: Riker sees the governors doing in the governed; I see all of us in it together.

Among the political puzzles of recent years has been the support shown for representatives by their constituents amid a general decline in esteem in Congress. Aside from the advantages of incumbency, citizens seem to have high regard for their representatives, returning them to office with increasing regularity. The explanation offered by Richard Fenno—congressmen support themselves by campaigning against Congress—cries out for extension. Why do both congressmen and their constituencies like what they do in the small but not in the large? Perhaps the puzzle may be pieced together by the observation that constituents are in fact getting what they want from their representatives, but what they want and get on each matter does not turn out to be what they want in total. And their representatives feel the same way. By realizing that in this respect all of us may be in the same boat, it becomes easier to accept the argument that choices on individual programs are not serving collective purposes.

What about the Congressional budget reform? It is superior to what it replaced but it is a modest, meliorative move rather than a radical reform. It does for Congress what the Budget Act of 1921 did for the executive branch, namely, helps get its act together. Its purpose is to increase the sense of self-mastery in Congress by making appropriations within a sense of total expenditures. Congress passes a first concurrent resolution, containing an approximation of this relationship, which is then modified to take account of decisions on individual items and which is codified in a second resolution whose total cannot be raised without special procedures. The budget process is now somewhat more orderly with running totals taken of decisions along the way. The Congressional Budget Office has improved the accuracy of budget numbers by providing a competitive source of expertise, and it has made competent analysis more widely available to those who want it. But (a big but) the Budget Act is not designed to serve as a one-way street to reduce expenditure. Congress is encouraged to consider totals, but it has no greater incentive than before to reduce these totals. Indeed, it is quite possible for legislators to vote to increase individual items and simultaneously to vote to lower the target totals. Old entitlements are entirely outside its jurisdiction, and it only need be notified of new ones. When Congress is so disposed, the Budget Act enables it to relate desired totals to individual appropriations. This is desirable. But it is not meant to be (and it is not) inevitable. As a close student of the reform recently summed up the evidence, "Congress expanded upon the fiscal policy of the President somewhat more with its budget process than without it."[12]

The truth must out: not everyone is devoted to lowering expenditure. There are those, and they are by no means few, who believe that current levels are too low. They may believe that stimulating the economy is desirable, that high employment should be traded off for high inflation, that distribution of services and income is a moral imperative or a political necessity. And, while they have not been as successful as they would wish, they have reached higher plateaus of expenditure than anyone dreamed of a generation ago. All sorts of new devices have been spawned—reimbursements for this, entitlements for that, low interest loans for the other—to keep the funds flowing. Nor is it only a single lower class that benefits: almost all of us gain from tax expenditures on mortgage interest or accelerated depreciation for industry or subsidies of infinite variety. The people itself is split into its paying and receiving selves, without always knowing which.

Perhaps the simplest explanation is the best: expenditure keeps going up because more people benefit from public distribution than from private production. So long as there are fewer people with high income who give and more with lower income who receive, politicians can always win votes by spending. The only thing wrong with this scheme is that it runs counter to the known facts. Since an unequal distribution of income has been with us from the very beginning, over two-hundred years ago, what has happened lately to make spending rise so swiftly? Why, in addition, do the very majorities supposed to be supporting spending also say they think it is too high? Possibly, in the future, they hope to benefit from being productive. Possibly they fear inflation, which is not good for poorer people. Possibly they are afraid the minority will not continue to produce if they keep raking in their share off the top. Whatever the reason, a majority interest in major redistribution explains neither the past nor the present, for income transfers would, on those grounds, be far greater and other (say military) expenditures far lower than, in fact, they are today.

Suppose spending is ingrained in American character; it feels too good to stop. Or suppose spending supports American culture, the indispensible lubricant for smoothing social relations. Spending, under this supposition, is not only undertaken in support of American values; public spending is in and of itself an American value. I do not doubt that if these hypotheses hold, expenditure limitation cannot last. The amendment will be repealed or it will go the way of the elitist provisions of the Electoral College that run counter to our democratic character, still around but always ignored.

The contrary condition—learning to like limitation—should, however, not be casually dismissed. Citizens may feel more secure. Politicians may discover they can resist unwanted pressures. Bureaucrats may be relieved at losing their bad-guy image. A combination of fiscal responsibility with social concern may be appealing to a variety of interests. Presidents and appropriations committees will play more important roles. There is something to be said for being different, for showing that the doctrine of "American exceptionalism" still applies, for being the unusual modern industrial democracy that slows the rise of spending and limits the relative size of the public sector. All of us have experienced changes we thought we would not like, only to discover that the doing was more appealing than the contemplating. Like the federal government, limiting expenditure may grow on us.

Restriction may be liberation. The "me too" generation may be better off saying "I do." Pity the poor bureaucrat. He knows his behavior, intended to be individually rational, will likely end up as collectively irrational. But with whom can he share his guilty secret? Now, after expenditure limitation, our carefree civil servant can be consumed with clientele interest, yet remain confident that his own behavior will not bust the budget. In his own interest, he will not only defend his own program but will attack others that prevent it from expanding. Saved from his worst self, Dr. Jekyll will frighten other bureaucrats while Mr. Hyde pursues his highly individualistic notion of the public interest.

No doubt there can be too much of a good thing. Expenditure limitation might be worth doing on a year-by-year basis yet still be excessive as a semipermanent stance. Is reliance on a constitutional amendment an example of overkill?

5

Why Amending the Constitution is Essential to Achieving Self-Control Through Self-Limitation of Expenditure

One of the sophisticated financial arrangements available at your neighborhood bank is "Christmas Savings." In this plan you are committed to regular weekly deposits until some date in November when all the money is there with accumulated interest to spend for Christmas. It doesn't accumulate quite as much interest as regular savings. The reason people accept less interest on Christmas savings is that the bank protects these funds a little more than it protects ordinary savings. Regular savings are reasonably well protected against robbery, embezzlement and insolvency; and insurance takes care of what protection cannot do. But there is one predator against whose ravages the bank is usually impotent—you. With a Christmas account, the bank assumes an obligation to create ceremonial and administrative barriers to protect your account from yourself.

Some people cheat on the withholding-tax forms they fill out for their employers. They understate their dependents, so that the Internal Revenue Service takes more than it deserves all year—a free loan from the taxpayer—in return for which the taxpayer gets a reduced shock the following April.

Many of us have little tricks we play on ourselves to make us do the things we ought to do or to keep us from the things we ought to foreswear. Sometimes we put things out of reach for the moment of temptation, sometimes we promise ourselves small rewards, and sometimes we surrender authority to a trustworthy friend who will police our calories or our cigarettes. We place the alarm clock across the room so we cannot turn it off without getting out of bed. People who are chronically late set their watches a few minutes ahead to deceive themselves.

—T. C. Schelling, "Economics, or the Art of Self-Management," *The American Economic Review,* 68, 2 (May 1978), 290.

JUST AS THERE are many ways of breaking windows but only a few of making glass, so there are many reasons not to put preferences into a constitutional amendment. It is permanent. It is flexible. And it may be unfair to social groups that are already disadvantaged. Before saying why there *should* be a constitutional amendment, therefore, I shall consider the reasons for believing that there should not.

The arguments against an amendment have been persuasively put by Lawrence Tribe of the Harvard Law School. Tribe's impassioned plea to the Legislature of the State of California deserves an extended statement and a careful response. He declares that

First, the Constitution embodies fundamental law and should not be made the instrument of specific social or economic policies —particularly when those policies could be effected more sensitively and realistically through congressional or executive action, within the existing constitutional framework.... To endure as a source of unity rather than division, the Constitution must embody only our most fundamental and lasting values—those that define the structures by which we govern ourselves, those proclaiming the human rights government must respect. As Justice Holmes wrote at the turn of the century, "a Constitution is not intended to embody a particular economic theory, whether of paternalism and the organic relation of the citizen to the state or of *laissez faire*."[1]

But unlike the ideals embodied in our Constitution, fiscal austerity—however sound as a current goal—speaks neither to the structure of government nor to the rights of the people.... Because the Constitution is meant to express fundamental law rather than particular policies, it should be amended only to modify fundamental law—not to accomplish policy goals. Thus Madison described the amendment process not as a mere alternative to the legislative mode, but as a means of correcting the "discovered faults" and "errors" in the Constitution. Needlessly amending the Constitution injures our political system at its core. If the amendment device is transformed into a fuzzy substitute for the more focused legislative process, not only will the lawmaking function of Congress be eroded, but the Constitution itself will lose its unique significance as the ultimate expression of fundamental and enduring national values.[2]

Let me begin with the unsupportable assertions—that the Constitution is not about economic matters and that it does not (with regrettable lapses) or should not concern itself with particular policies. (Charles Beard, the author of *An Economic Interpretation of the Constitution,* would turn in his grave!) Then I shall deal with the more difficult question of whether there are statutory alternatives, whether the expenditure limitation is fit to discuss in a constitution, and whether it embodies fundamental and lasting considerations.

The Constitution, as originally written and as amended, contains numerous economic doctrines and policies.[3] Dissatisfaction with monetary and debt policy under the Articles of Confederation spurred the devising of a wholly new document. The commerce clause, designed to prevent balkanization of trade by states, the prevention of duties on exports, the restricted issuance of money to the federal government, and numerous other provisions are centrally concerned with economic policy. How else could one interpret the ringing words of the Fifth Amendment: "No person shall be deprived of life, liberty, or property without due process of law; nor shall private property be taken for public use without just compensation." If the Constitution confounds or conjoins "life, liberty, or property," this may well be because the framers found them indissoluble and considered them not separately but together.

It is difficult to present the numerous Constitutional policies without simultaneously presenting the document. What are the prohibitions on "excessive bail," or the conditions for extradition, or the provision for the public debt, all of which could be accomplished by legislation if not by specific public policies?

WHY ALTERNATIVES ARE UNACCEPTABLE

Now for the tough ones. It is a settled principle of prudence that something that can be done in the ordinary way should be, without involving fundamental features of state or special procedures. My argument, therefore, is that no proposal for improving the process of public expenditures will keep public expenditure from continuously growing larger in relation to the private sector.

Some people say that exhortation will exorcize the ghost of spending past. By this I signify such efforts to improve the process of decision making as requiring projections of expenditure five years into the future, requiring recertification of programs every five years (sunset legislation), or calculating costs and benefits every year for every program from the ground up as if there were no past (zero-base budgeting). Exhortation is involved because all that is required is going through the motions. Multi-year projections have been mandatory for twenty years, for instance, without making a difference (presumably decision makers were to shrink back when they were faced with the bad news) and without most people knowing of their existence. All the law can do is to accomplish projections; it cannot make them accurate or, more important, relevant. To do that, in return for making accurate estimates, it would be necessary not only to impose an obligation but to give a reward, that is, agencies would receive assurance that if the present program were approved, future expenditures would be forthcoming.⁴ They would give accuracy and would get stability. Why would anyone play this one-sided game. If he is asked to stick out his neck only to have it cut off? ("Aha!" says the legislative Scrooge, "Another project to lop off, another hope to disappoint.") Of course, there may be no alternative.

Compared to expenditure limitation, so-called sunset laws are but pale reflections of the real thing. These laws, passed in a number of states and proposed in Congress, require that agencies expire after a number of years instead of continuing indefinitely, unless they receive an affirmative vote. Because sunset legislation does not get at the causes of continuance but only at its outward appearance, it fails to affect anything except small and defenseless units. Termination, as Robert Behn has written, requires a terminator.⁵ It requires political attack and political defense. None of this is forthcoming. The absurd assumption that government grows because no one looks deflects attention from deep-seated difficulties on the grounds they are due to inattention. Actually, attention is

focused on all significant agencies by those they affect. Since
there are so many agencies and programs, the whole exercise
becomes pro forma. Because no advice or incentive is given
on how to overcome entrenched interests, "Sunset Apprecia-
tion for Beginners" is a lousy course. Why should legislators
who spend all their waking hours establishing new programs
and defending old ones suddenly take the pledge? Expenditure limitation pits agencies and programs against each other;
sunset laws enable them to give one another the stamp of
approval.

A common claim made for zero-base budgeting and sunset
legislation is that they "force" or "compel" consideration of
the ultimate desirability of expenditures and of the priorities
among them. Not so. All that is mandatory is going through
the motions. For one thing, no one can figure out what the
world would be like if things were different. For another, the
type of actions implied—elimination of agencies and programs and drastic reduction in expenditure—runs counter to
the everyday actions of all the decision makers. In fact, far
more innovation and expansion takes place after these procedures are instituted than they eliminate or reduce. Even if
zero-base budgeting and sunset legislation were to be far more
successful than they are, and they have hardly any successes
to their credit, they would be running behind.[6] Since there are
no incentives to alter customary behavior, there is no reason
to believe that spending behavior will change. And it hasn't.

It could be argued that indexing taxes against inflation
would, by reducing the federal tax take, decrease the room
for spending maneuvers without producing unacceptably
high deficits. Or reducing tax rates in general could be said to
have much the same effect. Imagine, however, that external
events or internal miscalculation (the food stamp example
involves both) drive actual and proposed expenditures up,
that the unemployed are out of income, that North Yemen is
under attack, and so on. Who believes, contrary to all recent
experience, that there would be resistance to these pressures?

No way. Instead, either larger deficits would be justified (mainly, balancing the budget at full employment) or higher taxes would be imposed. True, indexing taxes would make the free ride of inflation—higher revenues without having to raise taxes—more expensive. But this is one-sided: efforts to index taxation would surely be accompanied by enhanced efforts to index expenditures; why should widows and orphans (or national defense for that matter) be treated worse than high-income taxpayers? The end result is likely to be a compromise—indexing both income taxes and a substantial proportion of expenditure—amounting to a return to the status quo ante (if everything is indexed no one changes relative position).

The discussion does, however, unearth a difference over the direction of causality in explaining expenditure increases. Is it that inflation or other forces drive revenues up, thus accommodating larger amounts of expenditure? Or is it that pressures for spending increase the demand for revenue? In the old days, no more than a quarter-century ago, spending was supposed to be limited because a Chancellor of the Exchequer in Britain or a Secretary of the Treasury in the United States, as well as their parties and political leadership, did not want to risk public opprobrium or retribution at the polls. The restraint, however, depended on Holmes's "major inarticulate premise," namely, that there shall be a balanced budget. Once that went out the window, once deficits became desirable under most conceivable conditions, the constraint on raising taxes became notably weaker. Larger deficits could substitute for higher taxes. Expenditures could be offered to gain votes either by raising taxes selectively or not at all. The purported political limit on raising taxes turns out to depend on informal norms against increasing spending. Can we reinstate the norms of the past in decisions on expenditure? Why not a moral reformation (taking the pledge against gorging on spending goodies that give us a budget-ache) rather than tampering with the Constitution?

IS ITEM-BY-ITEM INTELLIGENT?

Up till now I have not stated the most obvious and direct alternative to a constitutional expenditure limitation—acting intelligently on major items of expenditure. If you and I believe that expenditures are too high, the argument goes, we should say specifically which ones should be cut and how much. From this standpoint, a general injunction to keep within expenditure limits, without dealing with individual programs, is the height of irresponsibility. As Jude Wanniski wrote in the *Wall Street Journal,*

> The trouble with a constitutional amendment requiring a balanced budget [the stricture holds against expenditure limitation as well] is that it doesn't tell us how to do it, nor do its proponents confront the issue in these terms. Surely most of those aboard the bandwagon, if asked, would tell us they would slash federal spending. But then the public-opinion polls tell us that more than 95% of the American people want federal spending reduced. This bit of information, though, is also of no value. Each individual citizen wants spending cut according to a list of priorities. Some would cut defense spending, some social spending. Urban citizens would cut rural spending, and vice versa. It's the South against the North, the West against the East, sunbelt versus snowbelt, and so forth. But these priorities are already reflected in the voting patterns of the Congress, and still the budget is out of balance and has been for decades.[7]

Somehow, he seems to feel that if what we are doing doesn't work, we should do nothing else. But the questions Wanniski raises are crucial. Why a constitutional amendment if it escapes instead of grasps responsibility? Why an amendment if ordinary action is more efficacious?

If you want to cut expenditures, you must cut programs. Simply stated, these words have much to commend them. I know; I've used them myself. Talk about improving efficiency, reducing overlap or duplication, perfecting procedures, which may be valuable as far as it goes, ordinarily does not involve substantial sums that quickly cumulate into large savings. You only fool yourself if you think nibbling at the edges is a substitute for the main meal. True enough as far as it goes, truer than the alternative mentioned, true under the conditions considered, but not necessarily a timeless and uncircumstantial truth. I do not regret having gone along with it on minuscule matters but, as I have suggested and will now state directly, investigating individual items is misleading as a general guide to expenditure decision making.

Doesn't everyone do it that way? You do your best on each choice and then the best has been done. Not really. In the home or in business there is an expenditure constraint beyond which one cannot go. Not so in government, which prints its own money, or which can invade previously private preserves. Our complaint has not been that government spends all national income, for there is assuredly an outside limit for that, but that it takes too much.

CRITERIA FOR A CONSTITUTIONAL AMENDMENT

As good a statement as any on criteria for including rules for decision in a constitution is set forth by James Buchanan and Richard Wagner, who favor a balanced budget amendment. They write,

There are several qualities that any such rule must possess if it is to be effective. First of all, it must be relatively simple and straightforward, capable of being understood by members of the public. Highly sophisticated rules that might be fully understood only by an economist's priesthood can hardly qualify on this count alone. Secondly, an effective rule must be capable of offering clear criteria for adherence and for violation. Both the politicians and the public must be able readily to discern when the rule is being broken. Finally, and most importantly, the fiscal rule must reflect and express values held by the citizenry, for then adherence to the precepts of the rule may, to some extent, be regarded as sacrosanct. These three basic qualities add up to a requirement that any effective budgetary rule must be understood to "make sense" to the ordinary voter.[8]

The short amendment appears to meet the first two requirements. It is simple and it is clear. My main reason for preferring the short to the long version is precisely on these grounds. The short version sounds like an amendment and does not require the economic exegesis that would be necessary to interpret the anti-inflation formula. Compared to other more felicitous phrases, like "due process," "necessary and proper," "cruel and unusual," and "general welfare," poor, prosaic GNP is a veritable storehouse of certainty.

But would the amendment, as Tribe, Buchanan, and Wagner rightly ask, fit comfortably with the values of the American people? The easy answer, unfortunately too facile by far, is that this is exactly what the effort to amend the constitution is about. The hard place lies in the realization that an amendment may survive the process of ratification and yet, to revert to an earlier form of expression, be found alien to the genius of the people. Answering the question really calls for a projection: will the spending proclivities of the population prove long-lasting while the sober-sides saving syndrome withers on the vine? Or will restriction be revealed as rewarding, so that the institutional embodiment of expenditure limitation becomes integrated into the political personality of American life? Making these projections is tantamount to answering our fundamental inquiry: Why amend the Constitution to limit federal expenditures?

THE RATIONALE: CHANGING RESULTANTS INTO DECISIONS

This is the rationale for a constitutional amendment: not only a particular public policy at a point in time is being negotiated but a social contract into which no one will enter without some assurance it will last. The relative shares of the public and private sectors are fixed so that the private is protected from diminution and the public is guaranteed the availability of its share of the national product. If the alleged advantages are to be obtained, sacrifices must be symmetrical; I will sacrifice today because I know your turn will come tomorrow. (Put less pejoratively, there is no point in your sacrifice if I don't make mine, because the end result depends on both of us.) We must know that we are in this together to make it at all worthwhile. When it comes to cutting the federal budget, as Walter Mondale has observed, "Everybody is for it in general as long as it doesn't affect them specifically."[9] People must know, to paraphrase Franklin, that they are going to hang separately before they will be willing to hang together.

The rationale may be restated to reveal the steps involved in its reasoning. The people and their government, separately and collectively, make decisions that add up to larger expenditures than they think is appropriate. Rather than choose a number that must be divorced from reality, they prefer a relationship to national product so that the public and private sectors can join in this social contract: self-control through self-limitation of expenditures.

A constitutional amendment is being considered precisely because it is not an ordinary but an extraordinary rule, a rule that governs other rules. Such a rule is necessary because a social contract dividing the relative shares of the public and private sectors requires a solemn formulation and a secure resting place; for without expectation the rules will remain the same; few will play the expenditure game. A grand rule is also necessary in order accurately to reflect public opinion. Were substantial spending desired by strong and lasting majorities, the rules of the political game would permit this opinion to be registered in budgetary decision. But should there be an opposite opinion, reflecting a desire to slow down spending, it would not have an equal opportunity to manifest itself in the budget. Without the amendment there would be no way for slow spenders to get together to enforce equal sacrifice so that the general rule could become part and parcel of the calculus involved in individual spending decisions.

Most of the decisions that affect our lives are not directly decided by anyone. The distribution of income, the size of families, the location of residences, are not direct decisions but are indirect resultants of a variety of public and private choices that affect how we live, from pay scales in industry to welfare provisions by government, from tuition rates in college to aid to dependent children, from zoning laws to the cost of air conditioning. Changing a resultant into a decision, therefore, is of the highest importance, because it implies not one but a whole host of choices. After World War II, for instance, when it was decided that unemployment was not inevitable but manipulatable, public policy was never the same. Fixing the relative proportions of the public and private sectors means that many matters will never be the same again because they will be dealt with under different conditions.

FORCED TO BE FREE?

Here we have the modern resurgence of an ancient dilemma: Can mankind force itself to be free? Can there be freedom in restraint? Knowing our own weaknesses, can we decide in advance to bind ourselves against them? So did Ulysses chain himself to the mast so as not to be seduced by the Sirens. Unlike the crewmen, who plugged their ears so as not to be tempted at all, an alternative not permitted to modern self-conscious man, Ulysses allowed himself to hear and guarded himself against his all-too-human nature.[10] This may seem disproportionate when talking about an ordinary activity like budgeting (kitchen maids dreaming of kings), but it is concerned with the public virtue and the public economy, of which spending is already a third or more of all we do.

In his contemporary classic, "Essay on Bargaining," Thomas Schelling has argued that the ability to limit one's options may increase one's power. If inability to agree on joint action is mutually disastrous, for instance, as in the game of "chicken," the actor who can convince the other party that he is in a fixed position must win. Similarly, convincing the others that you are bound by a higher authority or have no bridges behind you may persuade them to capitulate. Because you cannot, they must. "How," Schelling asks, "does one person make another believe something? The answer depends importantly on the factual question, 'Is it true?' "[11] Saying so doesn't make it so, but looking it up in the Constitution and finding it there may make it come true.

When the (in)famous Hoot-Smalley Tariff was passed in 1930, it became evident that taking up tariffs one item at a time invariably led to higher levels. Exchange of favors led to most members' willingness to raise tariffs on the others' goods if the others would do the same. In 1934 Congress wisely decided not to vote directly on tariffs for each and every good. Today Congress grants general authority to negotiate tariff levels, which helps avoid (though it cannot guarantee against) the worst of logrolling. Why, then, can't we count on Congress to handle expenditures with the same wisdom on procedure it has so far shown on tariffs? For one thing, Congress has not yet tried to tangle with expenditures in this way. For another, tariffs turn on avoiding instant exchange of favors at a point in time, not over periods of time. Budgeting is continuous. Its problem is that that accumulation of choices over time adds up to too much. The solution to this problem is to face the legislature and those who work through it with a rule that already takes into account consequences over time. Unless I am much mistaken, this capacity to make the future part of the present is precisely the purpose of constitutional provisions.

Systems may still oscillate out of control if the governing principle in accord with which they coordinate their activities is either immoral or inappropriate. Limitation might be inappropriate if the constitutional provisions cannot prevent end runs, so that the nation is saddled with even larger spending and with even less control. Expenditure limitation might be rejected as immoral if it were to discriminate consistently against a majority of citizens or minorities who depend on government. I shall, therefore, look next at "End Runs" and then devote the last lecture to "Winners and Losers."

6

End Runs

THE DISTRIBUTION OF advantages and disadvantages from structural change is determined not by how it is supposed to work in theory but by how it actually does work in practice. No one is gifted with clairvoyance, but everyone knows that in so important a matter, persistent efforts will be made to avoid the limits. To the extent that these end runs are successful in circumventing expenditure constraints, they are part of the pattern of behavior that must be evaluated. Just as tax avoidance is part of tax payment, so escape from limitation is part of spending control.

TAX EXPENDITURES

Tax expenditures constitute any departure from the normal tax process that allows taxpayers to keep part of what they would ordinarily pay to Uncle Sam. For fiscal year 1978, tax expenditures were estimated at $124.4 billion, which would make up a substantial 26.2 percent of outlays. The largest items include the investment tax credit, deductions for interest on state and local bonds, personal deductions for interest paid on housing, and contributions to charity. In some instances, as Joseph Pechman and Robert Hartman observe, "for some budget functions tax expenditures exceed the amount of outlay: for example, commerce and transportation and revenue sharing." They go on to point out that the distributional effects of tax versus direct expenditures do differ, noting that "homeowner tax preferences provide little benefit to the poor, while housing allowances are concentrated at the lower end of the income scale."[1]

Controversy over tax expenditures continues unabated. Defenders ask why the government should assume it owns people's money. Why not support charity or home owning in this simple and effective way? Critics contend that these loopholes favor people in higher brackets who are able to move more of the government's money. If subsidies are desirable, they say, these preferences should compete with others in the appropriations process.

Once more expenditure limitation alters prior patterns of political preference. Up to this day, liberals tend to regard tax expenditures as illicit (though unfortunately legal) loopholes that should be shut off as soon as possible; conservatives, on the contrary, look at them either as letting people keep their own money or as a necessary adaptation to the complexity of modern life that requires many exceptions. After expenditure limitation, however, conservatives can confidently be expected to condemn tax expenditures as tax dodges, trying to accomplish indirectly through tax subsidies what could not be done through budgeting. Liberals, by contrast, worried about low expenditure, may begin to believe that one way to skin a cat is as good as another. Thwarted one way, they may attempt to entice private enterprise to do their bidding through offering relief from taxes. Is this a desirable use of taxation?

Few would object to the abstract argument that the legitimacy of the tax process (and the political system as well, I might add) would be enhanced under a simple structure with far fewer exceptions. The sine qua non for this type of tax reform, in my opinion, is generally lower tax rates, removing the incentive to get away from high ones. The question for us is whether expenditure limits will increase or decrease tax expenditures.

At first, the hydraulic analogy—water blocked one way will flow another—would appear to promise a veritable flood of tax expenditures. But it is not so simple or so easy. Expenditure limitation, as we know, will lead to a decline in the need for revenue. Since the surplus can only be used to decrease the national debt, the normal way for this decline to manifest itself would be in a reduction in rates, more at the lower end, perhaps, but across the board as well. Lower rates mean less incentive for tax shelters, tax preferences, tax loopholes of all kinds. The behavioral case will be weaker because the financial advantage will be so much smaller. The moral case for tax preferences will also be weaker because, in a context of general reduction, the necessity is less.

Imagine a politician turning the argument upside down: lower expenditures justify higher taxes so that rebates can be used for purposes for which direct expenditures are unavailable. I don't think this approach would be popular. Rather, I would expect tax reform to proceed along normative lines: a more progressive structure containing lower rates with fewer exceptions.

Suppose I am mistaken, as is (alas) always possible, and there are much higher tax rates with many more exceptions. Political forces that could get away with doing this could undoubtedly amend the Constitution in their favor, or make emergencies everyday affairs, or otherwise work their will.

In the worst of worlds, to sum up, we would have both higher tax rates and larger loopholes, with tax rebates becoming the major form of spending. The small fact that direct expenditures were limited would serve to hide the big picture in that total expenditures controlled by government would be greater than ever. Expenditure limitation would serve to bring the government (and the Constitution) into disrepute. In a better world, both expenditures and tax rates would not only be lower but fairer, more uniform, and more equitable.

CONTINGENCIES[2]

There would be no need to turn expenditures into reverse taxes if the definition or calculation of GNP could be expanded at will. This is unlikely. Though there is no way to guarantee this might not happen, once it is understood that consistency is more important than content, the proper procedure is self-evident. The expenditure limit should be computed for one year under the old method, after which the new method may be used until changed. So long as the base from which the limit is calculated remains constant, the percentage by which it is to be increased remains the same if the same method of computation of GNP is used.

Alternatively, emergencies could be declared and never ended, effectively removing any ceiling on spending. States of emergency in national defense, the record reveals, have a way of lasting beyond their time. Too true. There are two ways of reducing this all-too-human temptation to create emergencies when there are none. The first, adopted in the long amendment, provides that the base from which increases in expenditure are calculated would not reflect emergency outlays. Since there would be no assurance that these outlays would be continued, emergencies could not be used to continue permanent programs. The second reserves to Congress and the President the right to reduce outlays. Since each year is the base for the next, outlays enhanced by emergencies may be reduced in any year and the reduction carried over to future years until and unless increased again. As a way of life that can be depended upon, emergencies leave a great deal to be desired.

The short amendment allows emergency spending to be part of the following year's base expenditure. This is done for the sake of simplicity and to establish symmetry: no special provisions are required to restrict emergency outlays and the base can be enlarged as well as reduced by Congressional action, though going up takes two-thirds and going down takes a majority. Rather than reinforce the temptation to call continuous emergencies to keep initial spending going, I would go with the short amendment. Or it might be better to make a different kind of trade: the expenditure limit could not be lowered, so there need be no concern about a temporary reduction, but by the same token, emergency outlays would not constitute a permanent part of the base. In the last resort, there can be no final protection against endless emergencies. The amendment is proposed to perfect the political process, not to replace it.

External events could cause spending to occur as if the amendment did not exist. For the first time in modern American history, in November 1978, for example, domestic American policy has been determined by considerations of international finance. The rapid decline of the dollar, coupled with understandable refusal by Germany and Japan to inflate so that the United States would not have to deflate, has led to modest but real monetary and budgetary retraction. Should this continue, the United States might well be compelled to engage in deflationary policies (severely restricting the supply of money and the amount of spending) not unlike the British Sterling crises of the 1960s. Should external pressures lead to spending under the limit, the amendment would be there but would not actually be operative. The very fact that there is a spending limit, however, may serve to reassure holders of dollars. And, during the worst of the crunch, the limit may serve as a floor, giving opponents of deflation a benchmark from which to defend their position.

Attack from abroad or insurrection at home could also lead, if this is not a contradiction in terms, to a permanent state of emergency. Limitation might become an anachronism. So be it. History is contingency. No one expects to roll back the tides, and no one expects history to stand still just to accommodate a new amendment. In any event, the nation would be not worse off than it was before.

EXTRA-BUDGET OUTLAYS

An obvious temptation to circumvention—use of off-budget authorities, like the Federal Financing Bank, which attempt to lower the cost of federal lending activities—has been barred by the amendment. Expenditures of off-budget entities are counted as outlays. It is even possible that so-called negative outlays, like rents and royalties from the Outer Continental Shelf, amounting to several billion dollars a year, which are today treated as offsets to expenditure, may be reclassified as revenues. "This switch," Hartman and Pechman conclude, "may be desirable in that it would remove the temptation for the President or the Congress to manipulate the Outer Continental Shelf income estimates in order to hit a desired target level for total outlays." [3]

Of the approximately $12 billion in off-budget outlays for fiscal year 1980, around $11 billion belongs to the Federal Financing Board. [4] Obviously, when these substantial sums are included in the budget as outlays the totals will be calculated as if this had always been the practice. Thus there will be no need for an immediate $12 billion reduction, and this amount will be merged with the expenditure base. By the same reasoning, future additions to these outlays will come within the limits established by the amendment.

Something like $19 billion worth of enterprises, sponsored or assisted by the federal government, are outside the budget. There are seven sponsored credit entities, like the Federal Home Loan Bank Board, and several hundred corporations, that are either supposed to make money, like the National Railroad Passenger Corporation, or are entirely supported by federal appropriations, as is the Legal Services Corporation, or are somewhere in between, which would appear to describe the Consolidated Rail Corporation. Though they are either entirely or partly privately owned, these governmentally sponsored corporations are given certain special preferences and tax exemptions, as well as vital backing in securities markets, so they can borrow at rates barely higher than the Treasury and much lower than the private sector's prime rates that banks charge to their best customers. Accordingly, these entities are subject to some level of federal supervision. In fiction, securities issued by these entities disclaim federal responsibility for their liabilities; in fact they are listed in the financial section of newspapers under the title of "Government and agency bonds" and the government could hardly allow them to fail. Thus public responsibility, unlike private liability, is scarcely limited. Though their credit is guaranteed, however, supervision is not, since the executive and legislative branches do not exert direct control over their budget. Various attempts have been made to include these entities in the budget, but disagreement over whether it would be appropriate has led to no conclusive result.

Attempting to classify these off-budget activities on the basis of purpose served or rationale for public policy makes no sense. What they do have in common, in Murray Weidenbaum's words,

is that in each case the Congress has passed a law stipulating that some or all of their financial transactions are not included in the budget. The justification often given is that these programs will ultimately generate offsetting revenues and hence be no burden to the taxpayer. However, this rationale is of dubious value. First of all, those revenues may not always equal the off-budget outlays. And, secondly, many government programs which are included in the budget also generate offsetting receipts. Thus, the off-budget treatment is a subterfuge for understating the size of the budget and a mechanism for diluting the effectiveness of the budgetary review process.[5]

The thing to do, therefore, is to worry less about how to define off-budget activities and more about how to eliminate or convert them into outlays subject to budget scrutiny.

Since expanding government-supported private (or semiprivate) bodies runs counter to the spirit of the amendment, they could also be folded into the base for calculating expenditures, with increases added to or decreases subtracted from outlays in future years. About the worst that can happen is that these entities grow as they have been anyway; the best would be to focus attention on accounting for them properly so they do not continue to slip through our fingers. Before that can happen, however, the enormous expansion of government-guaranteed credit has to be considered.

How does around $440 billion (no, that is not an exaggeration) strike you? That is today's estimated total of loans (see table 3) on which the federal government has committed itself to pay all or part of the interest or principal should the borrower default. If the borrower pays, there is no apparent cost to the country: defaults made good by Uncle Sam are included in the budget as outlays. But this form of accounting is fundamentally flawed. Credit is as good as cash; the difference between higher market rates and lower rates with government guarantees constitutes a subsidy established by the credit of the United States Federal Government.

For the first time, in the 1980 budget, loan guarantees are listed in an appendix. And the Carter administration has suggested an annual limit. Allen Schick is right on target when he says that "even if such limits were established, one can anticipate that constitutional restrictions on direct budget outlays will generate pressure for circumvention by means of guarantees."[6] Since almost anything that can be done by direct outlays can also be done by loan guarantees, and these devices are on a par with Treasury borrowing as a means of creating money, thereby contributing to inflation, what can be done about them?

The onus should not be placed on the amendment. After all, the figures rose to an astounding level (without the blessings of the amendment or the need to get around any formal restriction on direct outlays). The converse would be more nearly correct. The amendment will generate much wider and more serious discussion of a runaway form of spending that most of us had no idea was already gigantic. Still, knowing and doing are not necessarily related. We must first try to

TABLE 3.

FEDERAL AND FEDERALLY ASSISTED CREDIT OUTSTANDING

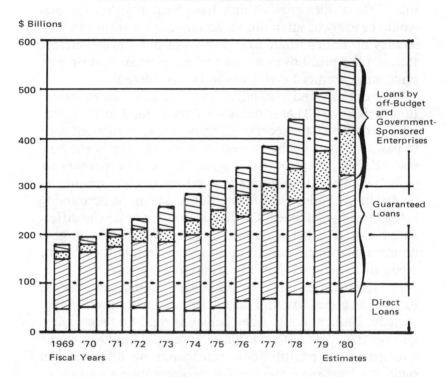

The funds advanced in a given year are simply the difference between the amount of loans outstanding at the beginning and at the end of that year. The accompanying chart shows the growth of Federal and federally-assisted credit outstanding in the last decade. Since 1969, the total amount of loans outstanding has risen by $263 billion, to $440 billion in 1978, an increase of 147%.

While most direct Federal outlays are subject to periodic review in both the executive and congressional budget processes, several direct lending programs are excluded from the budget outlay totals as are all loan guarantees, except for payments of claims on defaults, certain repurchases, interest subsidies, or other installment payments. As a result, the budget understates the extent of Government involvement in credit markets. In the interest of the development of a more rational credit policy, the administration OMB is proposing a new system for credit review and control.

Source: *Special Analyses,* Budget of the United States Government, Part F. Fiscal Year 1980.

answer another question, one that sounds absurdly simple: What is an outlay?

All along I have proceeded on the assumption that the real question about outlays is how large or small should they be, not what they are. I was afraid, to tell the truth, that a trip through these lectures might seem unnecessary if I began by confessing that outlays is a contested concept. Now, it is not as bad as all that. Listen to Allen Schick:

> The issue, at first glance, seems straightforward and without complication: an outlay occurs whenever the federal government makes a payment of funds. The issue, however, is not whether a payment constitutes an outlay, but how outlays are computed for budgetary purposes. It is in the counting of outlays that difficulties abound. *Grossing Versus Netting.* In the course of each year, the federal government makes a sizeable number of direct loans... and also receives payment from borrowers to whom loans were extended in previous years. The federal practice is to count direct loans in the budget on a net basis, that is the gross amount of new loans minus repayments. This method is consistent with the definition of outlays in the Congressional Budget Act as "expenditures and net lending of funds." The financial activities of public enterprise revolving funds also are reported in the budget on a net basis. These funds conduct business-type operations for which they obtain receipts from the users of their services. The receipts, however, are not computed in the budget as federal revenues, but offset the expenditures of the public enterprises. As a result of this accounting practice, the amount shown in the budget as outlays for public enterprise funds is the excess of their expenditures over revenues. In fiscal 1980, the gross outlays of the public enterprise funds will be about $46 billion, but with $38 billion in receipts from the public, the budget will show only approximately $8 billion in outlays.[7]

This compromise is creative. I would gladly settle for treating new credit as outlays.

Schick concludes that since "no constitutional restriction can be immunized against one form or another of budgeting legerdemain... the whole issue ought to be left for statutory determination where it would be decided anyway."[8] His argument is cogent, but I do not agree; the question is not only whether there will be statutes, surely there will, but whether they will be better or worse because of the amendment.

Statutes are essential. Constitutional provisions do not substitute for statutes. If that were so, constitutions would have to be comprehensive, covering all sorts of conditions that clutter them up without being able to anticipate anything like all that comes after them. But why stop there? Legislation itself is woefully insufficient. Statutes have to confine themselves to generalities, because they also cannot completely anticipate the future. That is why there are regulations, guidelines, even occasionally decisions. The growth of government can accurately be measured by the inch-by-inch expansion in the sheer size of regulations. Shall we eliminate statutes, then, because there is also a need for regulations? If the amendment is awful, this judgment must be based on its awful effects, not on an infinite regress in which amendments are no good because they require statutes, which are bad because they require regulations, which. . . .

Just as eternal vigilance is the price of liberty, and the Bill of Rights is not self-enforcing, so expenditure limits require dedicated supporters not only now but in the foreseeable future. Without continuing public support in a democracy, little can be accomplished. This essential support is far more likely to be forthcoming in the presence of an amendment dedicated to the task than in its absence.

As things stand, expenditures outside the budget—either not included at all or not counted as outlays—are running rampant. That things are bad does not, of course, mean that they cannot get worse. Unnoticed and unattended, except by a narrow band of specialists, as has been the practice in the past, extra-budget outlays, as we will call them, might well grow faster. Passage of the amendment will undoubtedly add fuel to the fire. But it should immediately be added that the amendment will also send up smoke signals. If the medium is the message, the amendment speaks out against extra-budget outlays, not only the ones that may come after but the billions that have gone before. Unaided by the amendment,

Congress and the President have not seen fit to pass expenditure limits or to enforce budgetary discipline by requiring outlays of all kinds to take their chances together. Now that we know how bad it has been, there is a better chance than before to do better.

The subsidies in loan guarantees (the difference between the cost of government and private credit) can be called outlays, which is what they are. Today these costs are passed on to unsuspecting borrowers in the form of higher interest rates or in restrictions on the amounts they can borrow, because government has preempted so substantial a proportion of available credit. Tomorrow, if we are wiser, the real costs to society will appear in the budget so these activities can compete on an equal basis with all other expenditures.

REGULATIONS

Squeezed by expenditure limitation, what is to stop government from requiring private parties to follow costly regulations either without recompense, or with tax credits or some other device enabling them to use tax money otherwise payable? Universal health insurance, costing over $100 billion a year, vast environmental and safety programs, all sorts of employment devices, can be guaranteed by government with little spending. All that is essential is to require employers to hire people, or to give a year's notice before firing, or to install safety equipment. Though this spending is not accounted for as government expenditure, the government is using the national product for its own purposes. What, if anything can or should be done to cover the costs of regulation as another form of spending that is not included in the budget?

The amendment contains a provision for keeping the states whole, in that expenditures required by federal regulations must be accompanied by federal monies. It would be desirable to protect industry in the same way, so that all measurable costs it incurs should be accounted for. But this path is tortuous, full of twists and turns and strange objects on which to stumble. Industry also imposes costs on others, from pollution to preventable accidents. Determining the amount of these costs and deciding who should pay for them are formidable tasks. Legal, political, administrative, and moral concerns are intertwined and no one can yet say they are well understood. Only the Great Accountant in the sky, who understands the endless ramifications of all things, can say what is properly public or private. What is to stop the amendment from making things worse?

Under expenditure limitation, allies are available who would otherwise remain uninterested in the costs of regulation. By tying spending and producing together, the amendment clarifies the close connection between distribution of benefits by government and growth of the economy. Billions spent for pollution represent a decline in potential growth that could otherwise have supported programs for people who are worse off than the rest of us. When welfare has got to be taken out of health and safety, coalitions will be created between industry and minorities that may well alter the outcomes of existing political processes.

Members of the budget and appropriations committees, when they realize what has happened, will discover that they have become immensely more influential. Limits mean that cuts as well as increases are necessary, and that is their function. The less back-door spending there is, the fewer the tax expenditures, trust funds, loans guarantees and regulations. The more all expenditures flow through their committees, the greater their power. Unless the appropriations committees stem the tide of back-door spending, their value as guardians of the front will fade into insignificance. By combining the second budget resolution with a midyear estimate of GNP, they can use the budget reform to reestablish their control over spending. It is a heady prospect.

Exhilarating also is the prospect of restorating Presidential powers. As the Chief Executive gave up supervision of individual items to specialize in macro-economic policy, he found that he had substituted a specious control over spending totals for the items that comprise them. The same complexity that inhibited Presidents before still operates. But, with limitation, agencies will have to carry more controversies to the President, because they collide more under expenditure limits. In brief, real resource allocation requires more central adjudication.

To be subject to regulation, moreover, an entity must already be in business and making money. Before there are golden eggs, there must be a goose. And a goose can be persuaded to go only so many places. Governmental policy would be placed in the hands of private industry. For some purposes, like mortgage guarantees, this may be perfect. For other purposes, such as safety, the prospect may be less pleasing. Conservatives will oppose using private corporations for public purposes because this confuses the essential division of labor in society. Liberals will dislike it because their programs will not be administered by their friends. The point is that most things cannot be done well, or as government would like, by telling industry to do them. Certainly, this is not a way to reduce the role of industry in American life.

Wait a minute! Regulations achieve benefits as well as cause costs. Surely, for purposes of proper accounting, the amount of benefits should be subtracted from the quantity of costs before the difference enters into the federal budget. No doubt there are benefits that belong in social accounts. But other federal expenditures, which do directly appear in the budget, also have benefits. It is these benefits, presumably, that justify expenditures. For financial purposes, however, for establishing the financial cost of government, it is precisely costs that ought to be counted. Spending by regulation is different from spending by bureaucracy in that costs are less countable, because they are absorbed into profits or prices, and less accountable, because they do not appear in the budget. On these grounds, there is more rather than less reason for the cost of regulations, insofar as these may be ascertained in financial terms, to appear in the budget. But what about benefits? Support should also be given to calculating benefits of governmental activities, but not so they can confuse calculation of costs in the budget.

ENFORCEMENT

The "coercive deficiency" was once a tried and true budgetary tactic; by arranging to run out of money for vital services toward the end of the fiscal year, agencies virtually compelled Congress to come up with the remainder. The Anti-Deficiency Act, requiring quarterly apportionments by central budget authorities, as well as other services, reduced the frequency with which the coercive deficiency was used. What, we may ask in regard to limitation, happens if a vital agency runs out of resources? Will the program be allowed to expire or will government have to rush in to provide the funds? Will government be able to do so if it cannot exceed the constitutional limit? Monitoring devices will have to be employed, including the usual periodic apportionments, to spot potential deficits early. A contingency fund may be maintained at the center to cover small unexpected developments. Spending targets may be set a little lower than the allowable limit so as not to go over. What happens, however, if spending goes over the limit?

How will the amendment be enforced? In the long amendment, members of Congress are given standing to sue the Secretary of the Treasury to act against violations. The short version, like the Heinz-Stone amendment, leaves enforcement, as has been the custom, to supporting legislation, which will have to balance it against overloading the courts. Based on experience with antideficiency legislation, the job can be done. Based on experience with the courts, the answer cannot be quite so conclusive.

JUDICIAL INTERPRETATION

The first cause for concern is that courts have grown accustomed to mandating spending. All along, of course, an individual's right to whatever he or she is entitled has been subject to adjudication. In recent years, however, rights to classes of expenditure appear to have emerged from interpretation of the constitution. Claiming that shocking conditions violate constitutional rights, courts have mandated extensive (and expensive) changes in prisons, mental institutions, and in other places and for other purposes. According to Gerald Frug, author of the leading article on the subject of "The Judicial Power of the Purse,"

> The principal practical reality that the courts must accept in shaping their remedies in the institution cases is that money is a constraint. They cannot continue their insistence on strict compliance regardless of the amount of money available, because the limits on government resources are no less applicable in the courtroom than outside of it.... A court cannot weigh the competing demands for government resources to determine how much can be raised for the institutions, nor should it try to force the legislature to raise the necessary money regardless of competing considerations. The judicial impact on the purse is acceptable only if the legislature retains its discretion to raise and allocate money, a discretion limited by the need to meet the judicial order but not eliminated by it.... A federal court's insistence on literal compliance with its own scheme ought to be recognized as having the potential to undermine, as well as to enhance, the executive's ability to improve conditions for institutionalized patients. Decisions mandating improved mental hospital facilities can divert money needed to deinstitutionalize patients and provide them with outpatient care. A new prison mandated by court order might be an undesirable substitute for small, community-based facilities.[9]

This pragmatic approach is admirable so long as the sums involved are not so large as to raise the question of whether there are any limits on judicial mandate of expenditure.

What happens if judges insist on spending which goes

beyond the constitutional limits or, more likely, requires replacement of other expenditures? Since I do not approve of judicial intervention in budgeting, I hope the amendment, by making it crystal clear that putting something in means taking something else out, will diminish this unfortunate practice. There are always programs that some people think have special merit, but this does not imply that our Constitution somehow confers upon them a preferred place. Aggrieved parties, who lose out because the judiciary mandates expenditures, would have good reason to pursue the matter. Ultimately, I presume that constitutional expenditure limits apply to judges as well as to ordinary mortals.

Of greater current concern is the possibility that the amendment might get bogged down in court where an unsympathetic or merely unwieldy judiciary would undermine its intent. The alarm has been sounded by former Solicitor General Robert Bork, a member of the committee that drafted the long amendment. Noting that the amendment provides for enforcement through the courts, Bork believes that though

> This provision avoids problems of multiplicity of lawsuits, judicial control of particular outlays, and the like . . . grounds for worry remain. The language and the subject matter are technical, so that almost endless opportunities for litigation, and hence for judicial dominance in the budget process, exist. Terms must be defined under endlessly varying circumstances; conventions about statistics, accounting, budget making and other arcane matters must be probed and specified. The prospect may be for nightmare litigation that would be damaging both to the judiciary and to the budgetary process.[10]

One hesitates to disagree with the Alexander M. Bickel, Professor of Public Law at Yale University, an authority of sufficient eminence to doubt the efficacy of his own handiwork. Perhaps, as Bork suggests, spending is so special that in this complex area the Constitution cannot save us from ourselves. Perhaps, also, a little lawyer-like distinction may lead to something less than a permanently pessimistic point of view.

Constitutions do not interpret themselves; judges do not select themselves. Armed with these unexceptional observations, it is apparent that expenditure limitation will have to take its chances in court. But by exaggerating its technicality as well as by underplaying its political sensitivity, Bork has misconstrued its vulnerability. The most technical provision of the long amendment, its formula to penalize inflation, is far more precise than most words, which can hardly be declared accurate to several decimal places. The only technical term in the short amendment is Gross National Product, which, as we have seen, is virtually tamperproof so long as its plain intent—that there be an overlap of a year when methods change so as to maintain consistency—is not subverted. Compared with amendments of some complexity, like the Equal Rights Amendment, which no one suggests abandoning because of inevitable disagreements over interpretation, the expenditure limitation amendment is a veritable model of certainty.

Suppose, however, it is not the courts but massive Congressional majorities that are intent on undermining the amendment. Suppose Congress were to alter its conceptions of what should be counted as outlays by excluding major items now covered. What could the courts do? Very little. The amendment is totally dependent on some support and on the absence of persistent political opposition. The purpose of the amendment, as bears repeating, is not to replace the political process but to perfect it. While expenditure limitation cannot work without being buttressed by long-lasting constitutional provisions, its purpose is to permit people to express preferences they already have for less spending, not to create preferences that never existed before. Today it is true that even if intense majorities desire lower levels of total governmental spending, they cannot consistently achieve that purpose. The amendment is designed to make this mass opinion effective; this opinion is its premise: if the political expression of public opinion under the amendment is for unlimited expenditure, the amendment is (and, in a democracy, should be) helpless to thwart that desire. Should the political process support spending limits, judges are likely to want what other people want. When there is a lack of correspondence between the courts and the country, the country will carry the day. The amendment hopes to guide public opinion, not to become a substitute for it.

Perhaps the task of enforcement will be done all too well by a resurgence of Presidential impounding. Someone has to enforce the amendment and, if others do not, the Chief Executive, acting through the Secretary of the Treasury, or some other high official, must. Overemphasis on impoundment as contributing to executive power would, however, be misplaced. The amendment makes all controllers of expenditure —the House and Senate Budget and Appropriations Committees, departmental budget officers, the Office of Management and Budget, the General Accounting Office—more important.

STATE SPENDING

It is also possible that stemming the federal tide will open up the floodgates of state spending.[11] Possible but not probable. The rapid rise of state and local expenditures in recent years is misleading in one respect: much (if not most) of it is due to transfers or matching grants from the federal government. Absent an increase in the federal effort, this impetus to state and local spending should also slacken. Within the programmatic uniformity induced by federal sponsorship, super spending cannot be sustained, for the states that take the lead will be disadvantaged in terms of taxes compared to those who hold back to keep rates down. The lesson of New York City in making itself uncompetitive, with high taxes driving out employment, has not been lost on others. To be sure, marginal increases may be in the cards. To the extent that this extra expenditure encourages states and cities to take different paths, it is part of the promise of federalism that states remain a reservoir of diversity.

The role of the states is relevant because the amendment does two things to restore their independence; it requires the federal government to reimburse them, using its own limited resources for any additional costs it imposes upon them; for a six-year period it also must receive the same share of federal funds as it is receiving now. Afterwards, however, the states and the federal government will have to renegotiate their financial relationship. Since there were states before there was a nation, representation by states is built into Congress. Accordingly, we can expect the federal government to assume certain expenditures, such as welfare, and the states to retain or discard others. For the first time in many years, state governments will be consulting their own taxing and spending preferences and priorities rather than doing things they otherwise would not except for the lure of "free" federal dollars. Artificial issues, like rebuilding the West Side Highway in New York City at a cost of around $2 billion, which no one would ever have thought of had federal money not been made available, will disappear from the public scene. And the diversity that was originally designed into American government will again have full rein.

The years it typically takes to pass a constitutional amendment allow ample time to ratchet up expenditures. Might spending move so high as to make further limitation moot? I doubt it. Current circumstances, especially double digit inflation and the deterioration of the value of the dollar, do not appear favorable. The rapid rise in revenues resulting from inflation, however, will increase sufficiently in the near future to allowing considerable expansion. Though spending might go up several percent, should passage be delayed for five years or so, it is unlikely to go higher. Presumably, the same people pushing passage would be able to prevent extraordinary increases above the proportionate growth of national product. Of course, there are those for whom any increase is anathema, who would like to drive down the share of governments at all levels in GNP. This is not my view. The past is full of dire predictions, should public expenditure grow beyond 5 percent to 25 percent of GNP. There is no need to join in the general hysteria. The important thing, in my opinion, is for federal expenditure to be limited by relation to GNP at not much higher a level than it is today.

REFRAIN

Why consider a constitutional amendment if not every conceivable consequence can be anticipated? Because I believe that the palpable good expenditure limitation would do outweighs the hypothetical evils it might encourage, evils that, like the cost of regulation, might be borne on the grounds that they are already with us. We are not talking about something new, but an intensification of something old and already disagreeable that will get worse even if expenditures are never limited. Expenditures flow out of so many faucets. It is not easy to argue that shutting off some will make the remainder sufficiently worse that it will increase the total take from the national product. If the end runs seem endless and limitless, it is cause for caution in approving the amendment, and it is cause for concern that all these devices should have been allowed to last so long and wax so fat. Consideration of end runs around the amendment hardly leads to nostalgia for the bad old days; consideration of end runs should lead instead to ways of mitigating, if not ending, the extra-budget expenditure runaround.

It could be argued, as Nat Cippolina has suggested, that there might be even less control over the end runs when they become the only means of increasing expenditures. Might special interests not become adept at concentrating their political and professional resources on controlling and influencing the end run or extra-budget expenditures? Might this remove Congress as the intermediary and make it even less important in the overall political system? At least now, the argument continues, spending interests have to appeal to congressmen. If they have to appeal only to treasury and off-budget pseudobureaucrats, congressmen would lose whatever mitigating influence they had had. I might take this more seriously if more than half the outlays were *not* already avoiding the appropriations process, and Congress were trying harder to recapture control over spending.

7

Winners and Losers

IT IS GENERALLY accepted among students of political processes that every way of doing things helps and hinders some people and purposes more than others. None can be neutral, for there is always an alternative that might produce different outcomes. Certainly electoral devices, party systems, and institutional arrangements are often spoken of in this way. Why, in this respect, should budgetary procedures be different? They are not. There is no reason, therefore, however reasonable present processes may be, why alternatives might not be considered that would have different (and perhaps more desirable) consequences.

People are free to do as I have done and make their own estimates of the distribution of advantages under the amendment. As a political scientist I enjoy this sport as much as anyone, but it ultimately remains a game whose outcome is uncertain. In addition to the usual uncertainties attendant on prediction in complicated social circumstances, perhaps leading the various actors to adjust in unsuspected ways, or possibly being determined by external events over which there is little control, outcomes have been left ambiguous. The amendment deliberately does not give preference to any kind of expenditure or any form of taxation, for if there were agreement on winners and losers in advance, it would be much more difficult to gain consent. A constitutional amendment, as opposed to legislation, seeks to sum outcomes over a long period of time, congeries of interests, and untold future circumstances. It would fail not only political but constitutional tests if it were possible to predict actual outcomes for individual interests far into the future.

Before we begin talking about winners and losers, as if expenditure were entirely a sport, it is well to consider the wise words of Benjamin Franklin as he urged his compatriots at the Constitutional Convention not to impose property qualifications upon voters in federal elections. Franklin is reported to have said that

It is of great consequence that we should not depress the virtue and public spirit of our common people; of which they displayed a great deal during the war, and which contributed principally to the favorable issue of it. He related the honorable refusal of the American seamen who were carried in great numbers into the British Prisons during the war, to redeem themselves from misery or to seek their fortunes, by entering on board the Ships of the Enemies to their Country; contrasting their patriotism with a contemporary instance in which the British seamen made prisoners by the Americans, readily entered on the ships of the latter on being promised a share to the prizes that might be made out of their own Country. This proceeded he said from the different manner in which the common people were treated in America and Great Britain.[1]

If I thought this legislation had a class or racial bias, I would not support it. Life deals enough blows to those who have less, without abetting this by constitutional amendment. Adding insult to injury is not my aim (though I would not put it past some to say that, nonetheless, it may be my accomplishment.) Besides, I believe that additional opportunities for advancement at the lower end of the economic scale will be created by expenditure limitation.

WELFARE AND DEFENSE

In a marvelous movie, a pool hall hustler, played by Paul
Newman, is told by mean man, George C. Scott, "You're a
born loser." Without much emendation, unfortunately, this
phrase could be applied to the feelings of most political elites
in the United States most of the time. That one's own side
has lost appears to be almost an article of faith. Small victories are immediately discounted as sops, as phenomena that
merely scratch the surface of underlying patterns of rejec-
tion. Conservatives know they have lost because the welfare
state, together with extensive regulation of the economy,
which they oppose, has grown by leaps and bounds. Liberals
know they have lost because their programs have been sub-
jected to sustained and (in the eyes of the public) successful
attack. One side is losing because it lost in the past and the
other because it is not gaining in the present. Nowhere does
this pervasive sense of loss emerge with greater clarity than
when elites are asked who will win or lose from a constitutional spending limit. Asking the question has the added
advantage of illuminating how people think our political system works.

According to my own informal and unscientific poll, there
is disagreement about gains and loss from limitation. Liberals will tell you that, forced into making this Draconian
choice, government will reduce spending on social welfare
and raise spending on defense. No government will be able to
resist the combination of cries that the nation is imperiled
from abroad and the claims of the all-too-powerful military-
industrial complex. Conservatives insist that the cries of the
indigent, whether deserving or deceitful, as well as the ever-
increasing number of beneficiaries from this subsidy or that,
will invariably triumph over the outnumbered and rather
remote requests of the military.[2] Apparently this is the best of
all possible worlds, because there is evidently a tacit agreement that each side will get what it wants—more for welfare

and more for defense—without raising the question of fitting within limits under which either might lose.

Who will be the victor getting the spoils when expenditures are limited to the present level plus the real increase in national product? Will it be defense or welfare or general governmental services? New programs or old ones? The older areas of the northeast and midwest or the newer ones along the western and southern sunbelt? Whites or blacks? Rich or poor? However you cut the cake, it is important to understand that three factors operating in the past will work just as strongly in the present—the political process has not been altered, the economy still matters, and the international arena is still dangerous. Indeed, at the extreme—war or worldwide economic dislocation—the amendment's emergency procedures suspend its expenditure limitations.

The very same political process that produces large and rapid increases in spending also operates to ensure that their distribution will be only moderately egalitarian, for the price of political consent is enlarging the program to include more beneficiaries who are not subject to the same strict qualifications.

The normal tendency of democratic politics to broaden benefits and broaden the tax base means that large programs are not likely to be markedly redistributive.

Though the trend has been running in favor of welfare, it may swing back to defense; what seems assured on the basis of past experience is that the bulk of expenditure will remain within these two categories. In plain language, there is no reason to believe that allocation of expenditures will differ drastically under an expenditure limit linked to growth in national product, because there is no reason to believe it will change the political process that produces this distribution.

The question of who benefits, therefore, might be turned around to ascertain whether there are differences in types of programs that will lead one kind or another to be more or less favored under expenditure limitation. And indeed there are. Welfare programs, especially social security, tend to be indexed against increases in wages or prices, or sometimes both, while defense programs are not. Welfare programs also tend to be entitlements, where everyone who qualifies must receive the specified benefits without regard to total cost, which is why they are also open-ended. Hence welfare programs are mostly called "uncontrollable," meaning the cost continues unless the basic legislation is altered, whereas defense is "controllable" in that it can be changed through the appropriations process. Defense, moreover, is determined one year at a time but welfare is treated as "multiyear" or "no year" that is, as going on indefinitely. One way of looking at this difference in type of program is that defense is disadvantaged; another way is that welfare ought to worry about the capping of its programs so they will become single-year, fixed-sum appropriations rather than multiyear, open-ended entitlements.

Here we have the main effect of expenditure limitation: it will encourage internal scrutiny not only of program content but of program growth over time. It will be evident to everyone that excessive growth in one program must be taken out of others. Much more explicit decisions will have to be made on how far and fast programs should go. The same, by the way, will hold for cost overruns on military hardware. Overruns will have to come out of the rest of the defense budget. Limitation will become a way of life.

But it is not in defense or welfare, which have strong roots in need and constituency, that I would expect the main impact of limitation to be felt. I refer to the super-subsidies for internal improvements in the maritime industry, for milk and tobacco, for the Post Office, and for the Corps of Engineers. All these will be forced into the spotlight. The total costs they incur will matter, since the more they spend, the less will be made available for others. For good or ill, who gets how much subsidy will be subject to sharp scrutiny. Somehow, I don't think that those who receive subsidies while engaged in commerce have the votes to take what they want from the elderly, the unemployed, and the poor minorities who depend on social welfare. The clearer the stakes and the more visible the arena (which would certainly describe the budgetary process under expenditure limitation), the more votes count as compared with monetary muscle.

Up to a point. Predictions are guesswork, not God's work. Always there are other factors and conditions to take into account. Business has few votes but it has more money. And, as Charles E. Lindblom has observed, business is essential in some ways that other interests are not. Jobs depend on business; so does taxation. Because government has an interest in enabling business to perform its economic functions, pleas that it may be driven out of operation are hard to resist.[3] The reason that broad outcomes of political processes tend to be stable over time is that all major interests have something going for them. If corporations control public policy, however, it is hard to explain why they are subject to so much regulation or such high taxation.[4]

Whether or not environmental or corporate concerns would be affected by the amendment depends on how the costs involved would be accounted for. All along the way, expenditure limitation raises questions of what are counted as costs and benefits and to whom these are charged. The United States uses a self-assessment tax system, for example, that results in most accounting expense being charged to the private sector. Were it to use governmental assessment, as many countries do, most of these accountants would work for the government. Yet in either case the accounting is done in response to governmental directives. Similarly, if government cleans up the environment it gets the bill, but if pollution is paid for by effluent charges, levied on discharge of contaminants at the source, private parties pay. It may confidently be predicted that the efforts of economists to persuade environmentalists to use effluent charges instead of bureaucratic regulation, hitherto resisted as placing a price on pollution, will pay off if there is constitutional expendi-limitation, for legal orders will count as public expenditures but effluent charges will remain on private books.

Judging whether the better or worse off are helped or hindered by expenditure limitation depends on estimates of how
the private economy and public agencies treat the people involved. It depends on whether securing for the private sector
its present proportion of national product will have a salu-
tory or a harmful effect on the future prospects of people
with low income. If one believes that upward mobility is a
myth that strips the poor naked before private power, expansion of the countervailing power of the public sector is indi-
cated. Unless, of course, that would be worse still. The price
of that help, however, is the extension of programs to include
people who do not properly belong, thus increasing total
costs without concentrating on the poorest people. My choice
is evident, because I believe that autonomous individuals are
able to determine whether they have problems and whether
solutions are acceptable. Such individuals are more likely to
be nurtured by a strong private sector. Trading work for welfare is bad public policy. I am against perpetuating poverty
on the grounds that the poor will not or cannot work (I hardly
know which is more derisive), so they require permanent protection. Make-work is no work at all; everyone knows that,
especially those who are supposed to be helped. It is not that
I don't think there are people who want help and for whom
governmental services may be appropriate. It is just that I
think more money will surely make professionals predomi-
nant in determining who have the problems for which they
think they have the solutions. Dependence is not just a problem for poor people, it has unfortunately become a solution
for those who profit.

The professions and the industries that live off of government may lose from limitation. There should be less work for
lawyers and accountants under a simplified tax structure
made possible by lower rates of taxes. Choosing between income and services to aid the poor, income is likely to win out,
leaving the service professionals to seek employment else-
where. Industries that hold out the tin cup to government will
have a harder time. All this, however, is relative to what

would happen without limitation. As things stand, aided by the expectation of maintaining its share, the economy will grow and with it government will grow in proportion, leaving opportunities for new ideas and new people to make good on them. But not so many and not so fast. Perhaps it would be possible to set a different limit so there would be more winners and fewer losers. Maybe, but I doubt it.

ARE WE CHOOSING THE RIGHT LIMIT?

Is there something sacrosanct about the present federal share of national product? Not at all, except when one tries to select another that would win widespread support. Starting much below its present level would cause considerable disruption, including going back on entitlements (public promises, really) to the elderly and poor, and drastically reducing the size of national defense. Taken together, defense and social welfare comprise around 65 percent of the budget, with 10 percent consisting of fixed charges (like the national debt and pensions for employees).[5] Obviously, the most severe reductions would have to come from the two largest categories and probably from both. Simultaneously renegotiating international alliances because the United States can no longer keep its commitments, or, in effect, requiring that the whole host of domestic accommodations, over a half century in the making, have to be bargained out again in a short space of time, would place an intolerable strain on the body politic. Just thinking about it is enough to make one want to lie down until the feeling passes. Raising the limit drastically would be worse than what we have now because it would encourage speedier spending up to that distant horizon. Thus any remotely feasible and effective limit must be somewhere near where we are now, plus or minus a few percent.

No one can say that the proposed limit is exactly right; the important thing is that within a few years the limit begins to bite so that the benefits of a financial constraint are obtained.

While too low a limit would make it difficult to change anything (reinforcing the worst policies of the past by permitting nothing except paring down) and too high a level would encourage spending for its own sake, a modest movement up in absolute size would encourage balance and stability while permitting change. The relative sizes of the public and private sectors would be fixed, subject only to adjustment by extraordinary majorities. Precipitous reductions would be unnecessary. Assuming real economic growth, encouraged by expenditure limitation, funds would be available to try new programs, which, should they prove successful, could be enlarged by reallocating resources from old programs. At a level of $600 billion and a real growth rate of 3 percent, which is close to historical experience, $18 billion in new money would be available. Most of it would go to expansion of old programs, leaving perhaps $3 to $6 billion for new ventures. Even at today's prices, this is enough for a few ventures. Since it would be surprising if our knowledge grew faster than a few percent a year, proportioning spending to understanding is not a bad idea.

Without denying that less spending might be desirable, participants in budgeting tell me they fear that real limits will lead to simple stultification: every program will be decreased proportionately. "No thought" will drive out "little thought." Budgeting will be automatic and arbitrary. Though this hypothesis is eminently reasonable, it does not describe the experience of the past as well as some think it does. Right now, in the absence of limitation, most reductions and increases are allocated by proportional "markups" or "markdowns." But significant reallocation has occurred between defense and welfare. Presumably practitioners feel that this amount of change will be decreased by limits on spending. Before replying, I should say that this argument—budgets only change at high levels—simply confirms the built-in spending bias of the present process.

In my opinion, limits will loosen the floodgates of change. If modest increases facilitate change, the amendment already permits them. If increases are not possible, change will not be inhibited but increased. The belief to the contrary is based on observations that agencies and their clientele demand (and receive!) budget enhancements to pay for permitting change in policy. They do this not only because payoffs are profitable but also because they are possible. Everyone knows there is more to be had. When everyone knows otherwise, agencies and their clientele will adjust. They will not see sense in asking for what no one can get. Rather they will be encouraged to operate efficiently, so as to get more out of the resources they have, to accept reduction with a sense of resignation that everyone is in the same situation, or to make a political push. Agencies will have to take a greater interest in each other's spending, because that is where future increases may have to come. Thus both the economic and political rationality of expenditures will be tested more severely at the margin, which, in a democracy, is as it should be.

SPENDING AND ECONOMIC MANAGEMENT

Government expands the economy by deficit financing: spending is increased and paid for by creating debt, which, under most conditions, increases the money supply. Tomorrow, after passage of the amendment, the governmental contribution to economic activity will be fueled by lower taxes, leaving resources in the population to buy goods and services or to go into savings, where it is converted into investment. Which of these approaches is best for lower and upper income classes? At first glance it appears that low income people will benefit from higher spending and high income people from lower taxes. And so they will, comparatively speaking, if they are involved only in a single episode. Actually, however, the sequence of events repeats itself during the course of undertaking countercyclical activities. Who benefits, over time, then, by spending without taxing in an effort to stimulate the economy?

Poor people and people on fixed incomes do not benefit from inflation; only richer people, who buy goods that gain in value faster than prices increase, stay ahead of inflation. But the spending solution is not supposed to support them. As so often happens, a device to help the masses ends up aiding the classes.

The Keynesian spending solution works only one way—up. But when expenditures are supposed to go down, encouraging saving to secure a surplus, something goes wrong. Past spending produces political forces so strong that future spending becomes selfsustaining. Spending rises, saving declines, and so does the economy. Instead of the poor gaining at the expense of the rich, or both doing better, everyone is worse off than he would have been.

In the past, the doctrine that "You never miss what you never had" worked against stopping spending on the grounds that it would reduce future income. Since no one ever experienced the higher growth that would have come from enhanced investment, because the money was used for other purposes, no one ever compared what might have been with what did happen. With direct limiting of expenditure, future incomes may indeed be realized and may thus receive rightful consideration in the political process.

All this, of course, will take place in the infamous long run, during which Keynes has apparently assured us we are all dead. Only an isolate would say that. You and I are sure to die. But the people of which we are a part live on. When the long run is not a century away but only twenty to thirty years, when it begins after World War II, perpetually higher spending to save the economy turns out to be a bad bargain.

Spending is a poor tool of short run fiscal policy. From the time spending goals work their way into the budgeting during the spring preview at the Office of Management and Budget, to the time money flows (or stands still), at least eighteen to twenty-four months have elapsed. This is not control but remote control. By that time, decision makers' minds, as well as the economy, may have changed three times over. And the immediate effects are exactly the opposite of those intended; when it is desired to decrease expenditures, they often increase in the short run to pay people severence and to cut off contracts; when it is desired to accelerate spending, it often slows for a while to tool up for the future, thus allowing current expenditures to decline. Fine tuning the economy, like working with a greasy hand on a slippery knob, is easier said than done.[6]

By looking strictly at the steps in the budgetary process, it does appear that spending totals play an important part. The budget is made not only from the ground up, via agency proposals, but from the top down, as the President and his economic advisers seek a number that will aid in managing the economy. Under the Budget Act of 1974, congressmen are also becoming more cognizant of setting totals in terms of economic policy. Even if these totals are set too late to matter for managing the economy, why suggest that an effective expenditure constraint for purposes of federal budgeting does not exist in practice? For many reasons. Under the dominant Keynesian doctrine of balancing the economy at full employment, totals are set so high they have little impact. After all, the totals are *not* set to limit spending over time, but to serve the economy in the next year, which is something else again. Since the totals are flexible, set to suit the times, every actor has reason to believe that his extra millions and billions may be accommodated. Thus no one need exercise constraint, especially as everyone else is not. Setting ceilings, of course, is not done in a vacuum but depends on what has happened before, such as the existence of entitlements, commitments, and political promises exceedingly difficult to change. Well over 90 percent of the budget, as all students of the subject know, is usually not subject to change. In hard times, this budgetary base is maintained; in easy times it is expanded. The result is a pattern of continuous increases only occasionally interrupted by maintance of the status quo. As the base grows, so do feasible totals. In the end, everyone involved can say he was subject to constraints on total spending; these so-called constraints will have limited items of expenditure not at all in the long run and only seldom in the short.

Varying the rhythm of spending, with its dazzling ups and downs, may win applause for the pianist but it is hard on the piano. There is nothing more permanent (think of aid to areas adversely impacted by military bases) than a temporary increase. And there is nothing so disorienting as not knowing how much an agency or program is likely to be able to spend from one year to the next. Why should program planning be sacrificed to smoothing out fluctuations in the economy if (a) the program may have a higher priority than the fluctuation, and (b) the effect on the economy is, at best, paltry and at worse perverse? Securing the stability of spending, sacrificing more money for a steadier supply, deserves attention. Rather than doing badly what it knows not how—speeding spending to the economy—the government would be better off doing what comes naturally—varying the tax take to suit the times.

SUBSIDIES

From the beginning of recorded history, efforts have been underway to improve the honesty and (later) the efficiency and (more recently) the effectiveness of governmental expenditures. For several centuries, roughly the sixteenth through the nineteenth, enormous efforts (rarely greeted with success within the century) were devoted to establishing budgetary norms. By the beginning of the twentieth century, a confluence of circumstances in Western Europe and the United States led to an unbroken series of victories for budget reformers. Economic growth, the influence of nationalism on the willingness to pay taxes, and belief in progress through science and technology combined to create the impression that the budgetary battles of the past had been won decisively, once and for all.[7] The jewels of budgeting, budgetary unity and comprehensiveness, came to be taken for granted. Reformers went on to narrower questions of executive leadership and the rationality of diverse objectives without realizing that their impregnable fortress had already begun to crumble.

A major purpose of constitutional expenditure limitation is to reinstate the objects of classical budgetary reform: all outlays as well as all revenues are to be included in a comprehensive series of accounts in the subject. Spending is to be based on considering priorities at the margins of these outlays. None, except possibly interest on the national debt, are sacrosanct in the sense that they are not included in the budget or cannot be changed through the legislative and appropriations processes. Anything or anyone may be subsidized so long as these sums are identified as such. Stated succinctly, budget reformers are in favor of budgeting: subsidies given through tax preferences or loan guarantees, or in any other way, should be re-routed through the budget as direct expenditures, termed outlays. On the assumption that the amendment will do what it is set up to do, we may well ask what sorts of people and purposes would be hindered or helped by raising subsidies to the budgetary surface.

According to Murray Weidenbaum, the bulk of tax expenditures (59 percent of the total in 1976) are received by middle and lower income people so that, by and large, they benefit from this end run. In my opinion, there are other ways of looking at the data that suggest a different conclusion. At a minimum, 41 percent goes to those in the upper income strata and to corporations. Surely, this is too large in that (a) it does not disproportionately benefit low income groups, and (b) the budgetary process would not produce so skewed a result. Taking the figures at face value, why should middle and upper class individuals reap special benefits from the tax process? If anything, taxes should result in greater not lesser equality.

Regulation also manifests class bias; it is paid for by everyone in terms of prices but the benefits belong to the regulated,

TABLE 4.

SUMMARY OF TAX EXPENDITURES, FISCAL YEAR 1976*
(IN BILLIONS OF DOLLARS)

	Amount	Percent of total
Estimated benefits to lower income groups	$17.9	19
Estimated benefits to middle income groups	38.6	40
Estimated benefits to upper income groups	15.9	17
Estimated benefits to corporations	22.9	24
Total	$95.3	100

*Source: Murray L. Weidenbaum, *The Case for Tax Loopholes* (Center for the Study of American Business, Washington University, St. Louis, September 1978), p. 5.

who are guaranteed against competition, to the regulators, including those they pay to intervene on behalf of "the public," and to the regulatees, who are protected against private risk with public money. The beneficiaries designated by these three R's, it turns out, are all from a higher class than those who pay the bills. Not only are the regulated richer than the general run of the population, but so are the regulators and the regulatees. Whether we are talking about corporate managers, governmental officials, or skilled workers (protected, say, against competition), they have gone to school longer, are healthier, and have higher incomes than the general population.

Loan guarantees, increasing by the hundreds of billions, constitute curious creatures. Though they do not quite resemble any known species, they also speak with an upper-class accent. Mortgage money and student loans do not ordinarily go the the welfare mother. Whether legal aid is worth more to the poor than to the lawyers who live off of them is not clear to me. Some of these subsidies undoubtedly would win out in open competition, but would all of them? Would their relative priority remain unchanged? Would anywhere from 20 to 40 percent of the nation's credit be absorbed by government loans? I doubt it.

The only estimate of who benefits from loan guarantees comes from Murray Weidenbaum, whose conclusions make sense:

The very nature of federal credit assistance is to create advantages for some groups of borrowers and disadvantages for others. The literature provides clear answers on who will tend to be rationed out in the process. It is unlikely to be the large well-known corporations or the U.S. Government. It is more likely to be state and local governments, medium-sized businesses, private mortgage borrowers not under the federal umbrella, and consumers, thereby contributing to additional economic and financial concentration in the United States. The competition for funds by rapidly expanding federal credit programs also increases the cost to the taxpayer by raising the interest rate at which the Treasury borrows its own funds. There has been a massive expansion in the size and relative importance of federal government credit demands over the past decade. In 1960, the federal share of funds raised in private capital markets, using the Federal Reserve System's flow-of-funds data, was about 12 percent. By 1970, the government's share had risen to 23 percent, and reached 36 percent in 1975.[8]

A good measure of government's ability to exert self-control would be a legislative limit on the amount of this subsidized credit.

THE PUBLIC AND THE PRIVATE

Why can't the private sector defend itself? If competition is a good thing, and the amendment is supposed to increase it within government, why can't the private sector compete on even terms without additional constitutional safeguards? In ending this discussion of winners and losers, it is appropriate to go back and ask why I believe that writing expenditure limitation into the constitution, thereby preventing the public from gaining on the private sector, is desirable.

In a capitalist country, which, in the main, America still is, the precarious position of the private sector requires some explanation. Whether the analysis is Marxist or pluralist, that is, whether it is argued that a ruling class saves itself by concessions in the form of welfare programs, or whether poorer voters get legislative preference over richer taxpayers, the result is the same: a growing welfare state within the confines of capitalism. What happens then is by now an old story: policies cultivate clientele who cultivate politicians who gain favor by trading votes for other policies until public spending outstrips economic growth. Business, to be sure, is not left out—it too is paid off—but it is left behind in that more must be taken from it than is returned to it in order to support the system of subsidies.

My meaning would be falsified, however, by this overemphasis on business and capital rather than on the private sector and its people. For the seminal subject, in my view, is why our public selves disadvantage our private selves. In our public roles we approve what is done piece by piece, but we reject the whole. Looking at the growth of government from the schizophrenic viewpoint of a divided self, admittedly an unusual perspective, the public sector is able to impose obligations on the private sector that remain unreciprocated. The public is ultimately authoritative; it is sovereign, the private is not. The public may impose costs on the private (for its own good, of course) that remain uncompensated. The public can log-roll, enchanging favors, because its purpose is to expand agreement on common concerns, but the private cannot without abandoning its reason for being—that is, its privacy. In industry this sort of behavior is called collusion, or price fixing, or monopoly, or something the public sector says is unlawful. Given the division of labor between the sectors, only the public sector can limit itself against encroachment on the private sector. Yet there is now no way in which even the public sector can decide to set relative shares with the private sector except by adding up the parts and coming to a total. To increase spending, no coordination is required; everyone just does his thing. To decrease spending, however, transaction costs far beyond the resources of any single saver are required; only government can create a constraint to which all are subject at the same time and in the same way for the foreseeable future. Constitutional expenditure limitation pays the costs of communication beyond the means of other participants in public spending.

Budgeting by addition, as we know, only adds up to more. That is why we want to enable the people in their public capacities to take a standing decision on the relative size of the sectors. Not to do so is not neutral; it is a decision in favor of addition in the public sector and subtraction only in the private sector.

REPRISE

Among the charges leveled against the amendment is that it represents "a vote of no confidence in representative government."[9] Not so. By impelling extra-budget outlays into the legislative process, the amendment aims to strengthen ordinary politics. The larger the proportion of public money that passes through the budget, the easier it is to make public policy visible to citizens. By enabling citizens to have a say in the relative size of the private and public sectors, they are able to participate in making a smaller number of more important decisions. Knowing what you are doing is a good recommendation for any public policy. By perfecting politics, by restoring a respected relationship between desirable programs and desired spending, constitutional expenditure limitation should increase the honor of participation in public life. And the disaffection of majorities who cannot understand why, in a democracy, their desire for lower spending is not effective, will decline. If the criterion for a democratic voting rule is that it allows diverse views, held long and strong, to manifest themselves, constitutional expenditure limitation performs a positive function.

No instrument of policy is good for all purposes and under all conditions, and constitutional expenditure limitation is no exception. There may be circumstances not yet envisaged for which it is unsatisfactory. There may be ways around it that have not yet been conceived. But it will serve to stabilize expectations without stultifying change. In a time when everything seems to be moving at once, a constitutional compact settling the relative sizes of the private and public sectors will stand us in good stead. Its moral messages will send signals throughout society. Government is here to help but not to overwhelm. To get more from government it is necessary to contribute more to society. You cannot get what you want from government without considering what your use of resources will do to others; they will see to that. Private endeavor will not receive the leftovers after government gets its share; private people will remain the main movers of American life. Coordinating their efforts around these expectations, Americans will better be able to explain to themselves where they stand in relation to government, how they stand for it, and why they are willing to stand by it.

ADDENDUM

"What," a friend writes, "ever became of muddling through—agreeing on means when one cannot agree on ends?" He goes on to say that "much of the budget conflict which is now muted would become explicit. Not only will the Amendment increase the conflict in Washington, it will set elements of society against each other across the country." My friend is too kind to say that the doctrine of expenditure limitation appears to him to be dramatically opposed to the description and prescription of incrementalism as expounded in *The Politics of the Budgetary Process*. Consistency does not concern me, I confess, but correct views do. It took some time for me to convince most people that most budgetary decisions most of the time were relatively small departures from the existing budgetary base. Presumably it is not my description that is called into question, but my defense of an incremental approach as desirable rationally, because it lessens the burden of calculation, and morally, because it mitigates conflict.

Yesteryear—the late 1950s and the early 1960s do have a musty aura about them—I was impressed with the considerable coordination accomplished in budgeting without central control. When presented with proposals for a centralized determination of priorities, therefore, I objected on the grounds that no one knew enough and that conflict would be exacerbated without gaining additional advantages over existing arrangements. My assertion that quick, small steps could accumulate rapidly into large changes was challenged on the grounds of its being a blind for conservatism. Now that this position is being acknowledged amid vastly greater expenditures produced by incremental processes, I am being taxed with turning against the truths of yesteryear.

Every process of decision takes place within a surrounding context of general rules that restrain the outer limits of its behavior. Before the mid-1960s, budgeting was subject to certain common understandings—budgets would be balanced, spending increases would be slow, and taxes would be moderate. These norms were no less powerful for being informal. When these norms weakened and then disappeared, spending ran rampant. This had not happened under the previous process. That it has happened means not that we ought to repeat ourselves, but that we ought to rethink older beliefs, perhaps appropriate for their time but no longer appropriate for ours.

Another word about conflict is in order. By bringing past conflicts explicitly into current decision, I thought (and still think) that devices like zero-base budgeting would overload the capacity to control conflict. Obviously I do not see expenditure limitation doing that or I would not recommend it (and along with it, the dissolution of the American Republic). What I do see is that multiplication of public spending far beyond anything foreseen a scant two decades ago has not noticeably reduced our domestic quarrels.

Indeed, except when threatened by spending limits, everyone acknowledges that conflict has increased because there is so much more to fight about. It is not the sheer amount of spending, however, but its open-ended character that increases conflict. For if it is supposed that everyone can have everything because there is always room for more, bitterness at being given only modest increases is bound to grow.

When all is said and done, the most common objection to expenditure limits is that they will freeze the existing distribution of winners and losers. Fixing the size, the argument goes, rigidifies the composition of the budget. Merely making this claim shows what we are up against: change has apparently become inconceivable unless it is tied to larger expenditure, not only absolutely but relative to the size of the economy. If public spending were 99 percent of GNP, could we not reorder our priorities unless we went to 100 percent? Is "better" or even "different" not possible without government growing "bigger"? The connection between size and progress is made by the use of a vocabulary of determinism—the vast bulk of expenditure, so we are told, is "uncontrollable." To say that, however, is to say that our government is uncontrollable, which, in an era of big government is to say that we-the-people are out of control as well. The purpose of constitutional expenditure limits is precisely to restore the reality of self-control to our government and thereby, as citizens, to our political lives.

Appendix A

A PROPOSED CONSTITUTIONAL AMENDMENT
TO LIMIT FEDERAL SPENDING

Prepared by The Federal Amendment Drafting Committee
Convened by The National Tax Limitation Committee

Section 1. To protect the people against excessive governmental burdens and to promote sound fiscal and monetary policies, total outlays of the Government of the United States shall be limited.

(a) Total outlays in any fiscal year shall not increase by a percentage greater than the percentage increase in nominal gross national product in the last calendar year ending prior to the beginning of said fiscal year. Total outlays shall include budget and off-budget outlays, and exclude redemptions of the public debt and emergency outlays.

(b) If inflation for the last calendar year ending prior to the beginning of any fiscal year is more than three per cent, the permissible percentage increase in total outlays for that fiscal year shall be reduced by one-fourth of the excess of inflation over three per cent. Inflation shall be measured by the difference between the percentage increase in nominal gross national product and the percentage increase in real gross national product.

Section 2. When, for any fiscal year, total revenues received by the Government of the United States exceed total outlays, the surplus shall be used to reduce the public debt of the United States until such debt is eliminated.

Section 3. Following declaration of an emergency by the President, Congress may authorize, by a two-thirds vote of both Houses, a specified amount of emergency outlays in excess of the limit for the current fiscal year.

Section 4. The limit on total outlays may be changed by a specified amount by a three-fourths vote of both Houses of Congress when approved by the Legislatures of a majority of the several States. The change shall become effective for the fiscal year following approval.

Section 5. For each of the first six fiscal years after ratification of this article, total grants to States and local governments shall not be a smaller fraction of total outlays than in the three fiscal years prior to the ratification of this article. Thereafter, if grants are less than that fraction of total outlays, the limit on total outlays shall be decreased by an equivalent amount.

Section 6. The Government of the United States shall not require, directly or indirectly, that States or local governments engage in additional or expanded activities without compensation equal to the necessary additional costs.

Section 7. This article may be enforced by one or more members of the Congress in an action brought in the United States District Court for the District of Columbia, and by no other persons. The action shall name as defendant the Treasurer of the United States, who shall have authority over outlays by any unit or agency of the Government of the United States when required by a court order enforcing the provisions of this article. The order of the court shall not specify the particular outlays to be made or reduced. Changes in outlays necessary to comply with the order of the court shall be made no later than the end of the third full fiscal year following the court order.

DISCUSSION

SECTION 1. THE BASIC LIMIT.

The basic limit on federal outlays has two parts. One part applies whenever inflation is 3 percent or less, the other part whenever inflation is more than 3 percent.

Inflation Three Percent or Less. If inflation is 3 percent or less, the federal government cannot increase its share of GNP. If, for example, GNP increases by 5 percent from one year to the next, then government spending cannot increase by more than 5 percent. Even if government spending increases by the maximum allowed— in this case 5 percent—its product merely remains constant.

An important feature of the limit is that it is a *linked* limit in which each year's limit depends on actual spending of the preceding year. This is the mechanism that permits the Congress gradually to reduce the government's share of the GNP. If, in any year, the Congress spends at a slower rate than the limit allows, that sets a new and lower base for future years.

Another important feature is the time difference between the fiscal year and the calendar year. GNP for any year is not available until some months after the end of the year. The difference in timing makes it possible to calculate the limit in ample time for the necessary budget process. For example, fiscal year 1980 starts in October 1979. The spending limit for that fiscal year would be based on the rate of economic growth during 1978. These data become available early in 1979, just at the moment the federal budgeting process for fiscal year 1980 is getting under way.

The time difference also has a countercyclical advantage. GNP increases most rapidly during a boom. This amendment permits the most rapid increase in government spending when the economy is generally over the boom and in a recession—that is, twenty-one months beyond the boom peak (twenty-one months is the interval between the start of a calendar year and the start of the succeeding fiscal year). And GNP increases most slowly during a recession. That brings about a slower increase in government spending twenty-one months later, when the economy is likely to be past the recession and entering the most rapid phase of the ensuing recovery.

Government spending is defined in this amendment as "total

outlays" in order to cover as fully as possible all spending by the government other than debt redemption. Because emergency outlays are excluded, the emergency provision in section three cannot be used to raise the limit for years following the emergency period.

Inflation More Than Three Percent. If inflation is more than 3 percent, spending still may rise, but the rate of growth will not be quite so fast as the rate of growth in nominal GNP. Congress, therefore, will have a strong incentive to reduce inflation, to hold down spending, and to cut any deficit. The 3 percent cushion provides ample room for unavoidable zigzags in inflation from year to year, and for errors in statistical measurement. At the same time, the inflation penalty in this section establishes a strong pressure for responsible management of the federal budget while not depriving Congress of the necessary flexibility in adjusting to changing conditions. A reduction in the government's share of GNP should be achieved gradually, to permit an orderly adjustment by employees, employers, consumers, and investors. This is why the spending limit is reduced gently—but steadily. Also: the higher the inflation rate, the greater the incentive for Congress to reduce inflation. For example, if real GNP goes up by 4 percent per year and the nominal GNP goes up by 11 percent, inflation is 7 percent. The permitted maximum increase in government spending would be 10 percent instead of 11 percent—a reduction of one-tenth. If nominal GNP goes up by 15 percent, inflation is 11 percent. The permitted maximum increase in government spending would be 13 percent, instead of 15 percent, a reduction of slightly more than one-eighth.

For simplicity, inflation is defined as the difference between the percentage increase in the current dollar value of the GNP and the percentage increase in the real GNP. This is arithmetically slightly different from the usual definition of inflation as the rate of change of the implicit price index. (See text of proposed amendment.)

SECTION 2. HANDLING OF SURPLUS.

This section simply makes explicit that any surplus must be used to reduce the debt of the United States. The section is fully consistent with current practices regarding management of the public debt. Once the debt is eliminated, this would permit further reductions in taxes.

SECTION 3. EMERGENCY PROVISION.

Any workable limitation on spending must provide for emergency situations, of which the obvious and the most extreme would be the outbreak of a major war. This amendment provides for such situations by building on present practice, under which the President declares an emergency and the Congress may then authorize expenditures in excess of the limit to meet the emergency. In order to deter the use of this provision to thwart the intent of the amendment, the amount of emergency outlays must be specified, the authority must expire at the end of each fiscal year and must be renewed if the need for emergency funds continues, and the emergency outlays may not be included in the base for calculating the spending limit for future years.

SECTION 4. PERMANENT CHANGE.

Because of the year-to-year "linkage" in the limit mechanism, a change in the limit for any single year will affect subsequent years. Such a change should be made only when it has widespread public support. This section, therefore, requires a three-fourths vote of both Houses of Congress plus approval by the legislatures of a majority of the states.

Though a "change" may, of course, be either an increase or a decrease, this section has to do primarily with increases. The reason is that a decrease for any current fiscal year can be achieved by a simple majority of both Houses of Congress voting total outlays below the permissible limit. However, this section makes it possible for a Congress to ask the states to approve decreases that will apply to one or more future years.

SECTION 5. PROTECTION OF GRANTS TO STATES AND
LOCAL GOVERNMENTS.

This section guarantees state and local governments their current share of federal spending for six years. Thereafter, it permits reductions in their share to take place but only if that reduces total federal spending dollar for dollar. It thus avoids any incentive for further concentration of spending in Washington at the expense of the state and local units of government.

SECTION 6. PROTECTION OF STATES AND LOCAL GOVERNMENTS AGAINST IMPOSED COSTS.

This section prevents the federal government from imposing costs on state and local governments without compensating them. This closes a loophole by which the limit on federal spending might be circumvented.

SECTION 7. METHOD OF ENFORCEMENT.

The public needs assurance that the spending limit will be enforced. The Judiciary is the established agency of the Government for enforcing the Constitution. At the same time, it is desirable not to abuse the courts with a multitude of nuisance suits. This section allows only Members of Congress to have standing to sue and concentrates these suits in the District of Columbia. Though citizens cannot sue individually, as would be desirable in principle, any of their representatives has standing to do so.

The Treasurer of the United States already is entrusted with the legal responsibility for disbursing federal monies. The Treasurer is now personally responsible for debts exceeding the debt limit. Hence, the Treasurer clearly seems to be the appropriate officer to be named as a defendant and to be charged with the responsibility of carrying out any resulting court order.

This section prohibits the court from specifying the particular outlays to be made or reduced. Such fiscal management is and should continue to be a legislative and executive responsibility. Congress may legislate which outlays the Treasurer shall reduce and by how much. Permitting any correction to be made over a three-year period provides more than enough flexibility.

For example, if the dollar value of GNP product goes up by 11 percent and real GNP goes up by 4 percent, the rate of change of the implicit price index would be calculated by dividing 1.11 by 1.04, giving an inflation rate of 6.73 percent, rather than subtracting 1.04 from 1.11, giving an inflation rate of 7 percent. As this example indicates, the two measures of inflation differ by a percentage equal to the rate of real growth. For 4 percent real growth, the inflation rate of 3 percent used in the amendment amounts to a rate of change of the implicit price index of 2.88 percent.

TABLE 1.

SIMULATION OF OPERATION OF LIMIT OVER TEN-YEAR PERIOD
WITH STABLE INFLATION OF 8 PERCENT

| Year | Percentage increase | | |
	Nominal GNP	Spending limit	Spending as percent of GNP
1	11.0	9.75	21.3
2	11.0	9.75	21.1
3	11.0	9.75	20.9
4	11.0	9.75	20.6
5	11.0	9.75	20.4
6	11.0	9.75	20.2
7	11.0	9.75	19.9
8	11.0	9.75	19.7
9	11.0	9.75	19.5
10	11.0	9.75	19.3

Assumptions:
    Growth in real GNP 3.0 percent.
    Growth in nominal GNP 11 percent.
    Spending assumed always equal to outlay limit.

Appendix B

The Short Amendment with comments and data by its author,
William A. Niskanen

Federal Spending Limit

NISKANEN ALTERNATIVE

Section 1. The percentage increase in total outlays in any fiscal
year shall not exceed the percentage increase in the
gross national product in the last calendar year ending
prior to the beginning of said fiscal year.

Section 2. Following the declaration of an emergency by the
President, Congress may authorize, by a two-thirds
vote of each House, a specific amount of outlays in
excess of the limit for the current fiscal year.

Section 3. For the first six fiscal years following ratification,
total grants-in-aid to states and local governments, as
a share of total outlays, shall not be reduced below
the share in the fiscal year in which this article is rati-
fied.

[*135*]

Section 4. States and local governments shall not be required to perform any new or expanded activities without compensation equal to the necessary additional costs.

13 March 1979

Aside from its brevity, this version differs from the NTLC [National Tax Limitation Committee] proposal in four substantive ways:

a. This version has an implicit penalty for increasing inflation but does not include the explicit penalty for a steady-state rate of inflation above 3 percent.

b. This version merges the emergency change and the permanent change provisions of the NTLC proposal in a way that permits the federal share of GNP to be reduced by a majority vote of Congress and to be increased by the President and two-thirds of Congress.

c. After six years, this version does not require the outlay limit to be reduced by an amount equal to the reduction in grants below the prior share of total outlays.

d. This version does not include any implementing provisions. Such provisions, including a change in the impoundment authority, would have to be spelled out in subsequent implementing legislation.

TABLE 2.

HISTORICAL EFFECT ON TOTAL OUTLAYS

Fiscal year	Total outlays		Percentage change		Percentage of GNP	
	Actual	Rule	Actual	Rule	Actual	Rule
68	$178.8				21.5	
69	184.5	$184.5	3.2	3.2	20.4	20.4
70	196.6	196.6	6.5	6.5	20.5	20.5
71	211.4	211.4	7.5	7.5	20.7	20.7
72	232.0	222.0	9.7	5.0	20.9	20.0
73	247.1	240.3	6.5	8.2	20.0	19.4
74	271.1	264.6	9.7	10.1	19.9	19.5
75	334.2	295.2	23.3	11.6	22.9	20.3
76	373.7	319.2	11.8	8.1	23.1	19.7
77	411.4	345.4	10.1	8.2	22.5	18.8
78	461.2	384.1	12.1	11.2	22.6	18.8
79	505.4	426.4	9.6	11.0	22.1	18.6
80	543.5	476.0	7.5	11.6	21.7	19.0

Actual numbers for FY79 and FY80 are Administration estimates in FY 80 budget.

Percentage of GNP under Rule based on actual GNP, assumes that nominal GNP is independent of total outlays.

Percentage of GNP under Rule for FY79 and FY80 based on Administration estimates of GNP in FY 80 budget.

Table 2 presents the historical effect on total outlays if this amendment had been first effective in FY 69. This amendment would have most constrained the rapid growth of total outlays in fiscal years 1972 and 1975-1977 but would have allowed a substantially larger increase in the FY 80 budget in a year that is expected to include a recession.

TABLE 3.

HISTORICAL EFFECT ON DEFICITS AND TOTAL DEBT

Fiscal year	Surplus/(deficit)		Total debt held by public	
	Actual	Rule	Actual	Rule
68			$290.6	
69	$ 3.2	$ 3.2	279.5	$279.5
70	(2.8)	(2.8)	284.9	284.9
71	(23.0)	(23.0)	304.3	304.3
72	(23.4)	(13.4)	323.8	313.8
73	(14.9)	(8.1)	343.0	326.2
74	(6.1)	0.3	346.1	322.9
75	(53.2)	(14.2)	396.9	334.7
76	(73.7)	(19.2)	480.3	363.6
77	(53.6)	12.4	551.8	369.1
78	(59.2)	17.9	610.9	351.1
79	(49.4)	29.6	650.9	312.1
80	(41.0)	26.6	689.9	283.5

Actual numbers for FY 79 and FY 80 are Administration estimates in FY 80 budget.

Estimates of surplus (deficit) under Rule based on actual revenues, assumes revenues are independent of total outlays.

Estimates of total debt under Rule based on actual debt minus cumulative difference between surplus (deficit).

Table 3 presents the historical effect on the surplus (deficit) and on the total federal debt held by the public if this amendment had been first effective in FY 69. This amendment would have substantially reduced the deficits from FY 1972-1976 and would have generated increasing surpluses starting in FY 1977. At the end of FY 1980, if the Administration's revenue estimates are realized, the total debt will be no higher than at the beginning of this period and will be only 41 percent of the amount now projected.

TABLE 4.

HISTORICAL EFFECT ON TOTAL OUTLAYS LESS INTEREST PAYMENTS

Fiscal year	Total outlays less interest		Percentage change		Percentage of GNP	
	Actual	Rule	Actual	Rule	Actual	Rule
68	$165.1				19.9	
69	168.8	$168.8	2.2	2.2	18.7	18.7
70	178.3	178.3	5.6	5.6	18.6	18.6
71	191.8	191.8	7.6	7.6	18.8	18.8
72	211.4	201.8	10.2	5.2	19.0	18.2
73	224.3	218.4	6.1	8.2	18.1	17.6
74	243.0	238.2	8.3	9.1	17.9	17.5
75	303.0	267.9	24.8	12.5	20.8	18.4
76	339.2	291.7	11.8	8.9	20.9	18.0
77	373.4	318.4	10.1	9.2	20.4	17.4
78	417.2	356.8	11.7	12.1	20.4	17.5
79	452.6	398.6	8.5	11.7	19.8	17.4
80	486.5	450.7	7.5	13.1	19.4	18.0

Actual numbers for FY 79 and FY 80 are Administration estimates in FY 80 budget.

Estimates of interest payments under Rule based on estimated average total debt held by public during each fiscal year, assuming no effect of total debt on interest rates.

Estimates of percentage of GNP under Rule based on actual GNP, assuming that nominal GNP is independent of total outlays. Estimates for FY 79 and FY 80 based on Administration estimates of GNP in FY 80 budget.

Table 4 presents the historical effect on total outlays less interest payments if the amendment had been first effective in FY 1969, assuming no effect of federal borrowing on interest rates. This amendment would have allowed FY 1980 outlays less interest payments equal to 93 percent of that proposed by the Administration and, in general, a more countercyclical variation in these outlays.

TABLE 5.

PROSPECTIVE EFFECT OF INFLATION UNDER RULE

Year	Real GNP	Implicit deflator	Total outlays	Percentage of GNP
	(Percentage change in calendar year)		(Fiscal year)	
Increasing inflation				
1978	3.9	7.4		
1979	3.0	8.0		
1980	3.0	9.0	$ 543.5	21.3
1981	3.0	10.0	604.6	21.0
1982	3.0	11.0	678.8	20.7
1983	3.0	12.0	769.1	20.3
1984	3.0	12.0	879.3	20.1
1985	3.0	12.0	1,014.3	20.1
Decreasing inflation				
1978	3.9	7.8		
1979	3.0	8.0		
1980	3.0	7.0	$ 543.5	21.6
1981	3.0	6.0	604.6	22.0
1982	3.0	5.0	666.3	22.3
1983	3.0	4.0	727.5	22.7
1984	3.0	4.0	786.8	22.9
1985	3.0	4.0	842.8	22.9

Table 5 presents the prospective effect of the implicit inflation penalty at a constant rate of real GNP growth. A 4 percentage point increase in the inflation rate from calendar year 1979 through 1983 would reduce the federal share of GNP from 21 percent in FY 1981 to 20.1 percent in FY 1984. Similarly, a 4 percentage point reduction in the inflation rate from calendar year 1979 through 1983 would permit an increase in the federal share of GNP from 22 percent in FY 1981 to 22.9 percent in FY 1984. This assures that the claimants on federal spending always have an incentive to reduce inflation, even in the absence of an explicit penalty for a steady-state rate of inflation.

TABLE 6.

PROSPECTIVE EFFECT OF CYCLICAL CHANGE IN REAL GNP UNDER RULE

Year	Real GNP	Implicit deflator	Total outlays	Percentage of GNP
	(Percentage change in calendar year)		(Fiscal year)	
1978	3.9	7.4		
1979	3.0	8.0		
1980	-1.0	8.0	$543.5	22.1
1981	6.0	8.0	604.6	21.9
1982	4.0	8.0	646.4	20.7
1983	3.0	8.0	740.0	21.3
1984	-1.0	8.0	831.2	23.2
1985	6.0	8.0	924.6	21.8

Table 6 presents the prospective effect of cyclical variations in real GNP at a constant rate of inflation. Given this pattern of real GNP changes, similar to the present cycle, the federal share of GNP would be 20.7 percent in the middle year of the recovery period and 23.2 percent in the recession year, a 2.5 percentage point countercyclical variation.

TABLE 7.

PROSPECTIVE EFFECT OF A TYPICAL CYCLE UNDER RULE

Year	Real GNP	Implicit deflator	Total outlays	Percentage of GNP
	(Percentage change in calendar year)		(Fiscal year)	
1978	3.9	7.4		
1979	3.0	8.0		
1980	-1.0	7.0	$543.5	22.1
1981	6.0	6.0	604.6	21.9
1982	4.0	7.0	640.4	20.5
1983	3.0	8.0	719.6	20.7
1984	-1.0	7.0	800.8	22.4
1985	6.0	6.0	890.8	21.0

Table 7 presents the prospective effect of a typical cycle, with variations in both real GNP growth and inflation similar to the present cycle. Given this pattern, the federal share of GNP would be 20.5 percent in the middle year of the recovery period and 22.4 percent in the recession year, a 1.9 percent countercyclical variation. In general, the smaller the cyclical variations in nominal GNP, the smaller the countercyclical variations in the federal share of GNP.

Appendix C

PROBLEMS IN IMPLEMENTING
GOVERNMENT EXPENDITURE LIMITATIONS

Naomi Caiden

IT IS REMARKABLY difficult to frame laws so that they work in practice exactly the way they were intended. Often the more elaborate the regulations, the more ingenious are the ways found around them. On the face of it, limitations on government expenditures seem relatively easy to implement. One sets a limit and presto—no one can spend beyond it! But in fact there are a number of problems in implementing expenditure limitations, as those jurisdictions that have passed them are beginning to find out. Some of these problems may be resolved without difficulty; others may totally undermine the intent of the laws. This appendix examines some of the problems that have arisen so far in implementing expenditure limitations in the United States, mostly at state level, but also in some local jurisdictions.

EXPENDITURE LIMITATIONS ON STATE AND LOCAL GOVERNMENTS

Traditionally, it had been supposed that state and local government expenditure would be adequately constrained by prohibitions on state deficits which effectively mandated balanced budgets in all but three states.[1] These restrictions dated from periods of default in the nineteenth century, and as time went on were supplemented in some cases by additional constraints on property tax *rates,* which prevented taxes on property rising above a certain rate.[2] In some areas local expenditure limitations were also enacted. In 1923, for example, Arizona cities and counties were prevented from raising revenues or expenditures more than 10 percent over the previous year's adopted budget, while school districts were limited to 7 percent. Colorado also had a 7 percent local budget growth limitation. But it was not until the early 1970s that a serious movement began to limit state and local expenditures. In 1973 an attempt in California to amend the constitution to limit expenditures to 7 percent of personal income was defeated in an electoral ballot, and an almost identical amendment in Arizona the following year was also rejected. Similar measures were defeated by voters in Michigan, Montana, Utah, and Florida in 1976. Meanwhile the effects of the 1974-75 recession had brought about crises in government financing in the states of New York and New Jersey. In New York, the governor carried out heavy retrenchments involving seven- to eight-thousand layoffs, and on his own authority he placed expenditure controls on agencies, limiting increases to the average rate of economic growth in the state (that is, 3 to 4 percent annually). In New Jersey, limitations on both state and local expenditures were enacted by statute. To ensure that a new state income tax, dedicated to state aid and local property tax relief, was not used indirectly to finance larger state government operations, the annual increase in state spending was limited to the growth of personal income in the state, and local governments were restricted to 5 percent growth in expenditures.[3]

By this time, the tax revolt was gathering momentum. Between 1970 and the beginning of 1977, fourteen states and the District of Columbia had enacted some form of new statutory control on local taxing and spending powers, restricting the growth of property tax levies to some specified annual increase.[4] Then in Colorado in the spring of 1977, an amendment limiting annual state expenditure growth to 7 percent was added to a bill on property tax relief. The Kadlecek amendment, sponsored by a Democrat in a Republican legislature, came as a complete surprise. Its purpose was to use excess state revenues for property tax relief, and it passed virtually unopposed.

The mood of the country had changed. In the following year no less than five states passed constitutional expenditure limitations. In March 1978, Tennessee voters approved a constitutional amendment limiting the annual growth in state expenditures to the estimated rate of growth in the state's economy. In November 1978, voters in Texas and Hawaii passed similar amendments, Michigan froze the rate of growth of state revenues and expenditures, and Arizona limited state spending to 7 percent of personal income in the state. The Michigan and Texas amendments also included limitations on local government taxing and spending. It is interesting that on the same date Colorado voters rejected a constitutional amendment that would have tied growth in state expenditures to growth in the consumer price index. Finally, in November 1979 in California the Gann amendment was passed restricting state and local expenditures to the level of the previous year plus an allowance for population growth and inflation.

These measures were similar in aim. They were a response to "the genuine concern of taxpayers that the costs of government should not consume an increasing proportion of their income."[5] As the framers of the Michigan amendment put it, the spirit of the times was the tax revolt. Their intention was "to put the total collar size of the public sector under direct popular democracy while retaining the best features of representative democracy."[6] They wanted to reduce tax burdens and curb government growth, and to ensure that this really did happen, the design of the amendments became more elaborate as time went on.

The older measures were the simplest, basing the annual growth in general for expenditures on the previous year's budget. Later efforts generally tried to be more inclusive, and to incorporate an element of flexibility by tying government expenditures to an economic indicator. Briefly, most limitations included three major components: a definition of the kinds of expenditure to be included under the limitation, an economic indicator to which expenditure was to be adjusted, and a formula by which to calculate permissible expenditures.

Definition of Expenditure

New Jersey, Colorado and Hawaii restrict operation of the limitation to expenditures from the general fund. Local expenditure limitations in New Jersey, Colorado, Arizona, and the city of San Diego also apply to the general fund. Amendments in Arizona, Tennessee, and Michigan include all appropriations from state tax revenues. In California the limitation covers total annual appropriations of the state and each local government.

Economic Indicator

With the exception of Colorado (which uses the previous year's general fund expenditure), state expenditure limitations link state government expenditures with an indicator of economic growth. Arizona and Michigan relate government expenditures to a fixed ratio of personal income. New Jersey uses the rate of growth of per capita income in the previous financial year. In California the Gann amendment relates government expenditures to rises in population growth estimated by a method determined by the legislature, and to the rate of inflation as measured by the United States consumer price index or to the growth in personal income, whichever is lower. In Tennessee, Hawaii, and Texas establishment of the indicator of economic growth is left to the legislature. Tennessee opts for the annual percentage increase in personal income, but the issue has not yet been resolved in the other two states. Personal income is generally favored because it reflects economic growth, inflation, and population increase.

Formula for Adjustment

The simplest formula is that of Colorado, which allows state general fund expenditures to rise only 7 percent over those of the previous year. Arizona restricts state government spending to 7 percent of state personal income. In California, spending in any jurisdiction is limited to the expenditure of the previous year adjusted for population growth and inflation, with the year 1978-79 as a base year for calculations.

The other states have adopted more complicated procedures. In New Jersey, the formula is most easily understood by reference to a specific year. In 1979-80, for example, the maximum appropriation is calculated by "multiplying the rate of growth in the State per capita personal income between the second calendar quarter of 1977 and the second calendar quarter of 1978 by the appropriation of the State in the base year (fiscal year 1978/9)."[7]

In Michigan, the limit is equivalent to "the product of the ratio of total state revenues in fiscal year 1978-1979 divided by the personal income of Michigan in either the prior calendar year or the average of personal income of Michigan in the previous three calendar years, whichever is greater."[8] The intention is to freeze state revenues to their current proportion of state personal income. In Tennessee, expenditure growth is limited to the rate of projected growth of personal income in the calendar year in which the fiscal year begins. Finally, San Diego's limit allows an increase equivalent to three-quarters of the percentage change in the price index added to the percentage increase in population growth. Each of these variations presents its own peculiar problems in implementation.

IMPLEMENTING EXPENDITURE LIMITATIONS

Apart from the aforementioned local government limits and the state of New York, where the situation has been more fluid because of lack of a statutory or constitutional instrument, there has been little experience in implementing expenditure limitation. It is difficult to generalize about their restrictiveness so far.[9] There is a feeling that these limits have not yet exerted serious pressure on government spending. Most have been deliberately set at about or below the current rate of budget increase. For example, in Michigan, the state government has been living within the limit for the past five years. In Tennessee, there is some doubt whether state government expenditure will ever reach the constitutional limit because revenue constraints are so great. In other states, such as Arizona and New Jersey, cuts in appropriations would have been made even without the limitation as a matter of policy, so that while the limitation has strengthened their rationale, it has not really been responsible for them.

In California, the probable impact of the Gann amendment is heavily influenced by changes in the revenue position brought about by Proposition Thirteen and the measures adopted to alleviate it, and by future uncertainties surrounding the possible passage of a new amendment placed on the ballot for June 1980 by Howard

Jarvis. The immediate effects on local governments of the 55 percent cut in property taxes caused by Proposition Thirteen were mitigated by replacement of revenues from state surplus, the use of reserves, and deferment of salary increases and capital maintenance. Aggregate expenditures in 1978-79 actually increased over the previous year, but in certain areas spending was reduced and the increases that did take place were below the level of inflation.[10] But in future years it seems unlikely that even these levels of spending can be maintained without state tax increases. It has been estimated that the Gann amendment will cause a further loss of $3.4 billion in local revenues and $2.2 billion in state revenues in its first year of operation,[11] but these figures depend on estimates of the performance of the California economy—a mild recession would probably force revenues below the Gann expenditure ceilings.[12] A further complication arises from the legislation adopted in June 1979 for a long term state financing plan for local government. This requires a cut, or "deflator reduction," in state subventions to local authorities if estimated state revenues should fall below a certain sum. According to current revenue estimates, this deflator may well come into operation in 1980-81, further depressing local government resources. If the Jarvis amendment were to pass, however, its impact would dwarf that of the Gann amendment. It would cut personal income taxes to half the 1978 rate, would fully index personal income taxes, and would exempt business inventories from property tax, immediately reducing state revenues by $5.1 billion and local revenues by $500 million.

In future years, the limitations are likely to exercise much greater restraint on state government expenditures. For example, Colorado's rigid limit is likely to put state government spending well below the rate of inflation, and it has been estimated that it will decline in real terms by about 10 percent annually over the next few years. Although links with personal income in other states may compensate to some extent for inflation and population growth, their real spending power will probably deteriorate. When this happens, unless changes are made in the limitations it is likely that politicians and officials will look for means of evasion. The possibilities open to them depend on the precise wording of the measures. The following seven "cracks" have already been discovered, and undoubtedly others will be found.

The Escape Exit

The most straightforward and legitimate way of avoiding an expenditure limitation is to use the formal escape clauses set out in the constitutional amendments. The most liberal of these is contained in the Tennessee amendment. The General Assembly may override the limitation by a simple majority in a special bill which sets out the dollar amount and rate by which the limitation may be exceeded. This is a "full disclosure procedure," designed to emphasize "brighter spotlights, not fiscal handcuffs."[13]

Other states have been less sanguine. In Texas, the legislature must declare an emergency by record vote. In Arizona and Hawaii, a two-thirds majority of each house of the legislature is required. In Michigan, the governor must request the legislature to declare an emergency and state its nature, dollar amount, and the method whereby it will be funded. The declaration must be passed by a two-thirds majority of the members elected and serving in each house. In California, emergencies may be declared by a two-thirds vote of the legislature or local governing body and are unlimited in duration, but there is a requirement that crisis funds spent over the regular limit must be repaid over the next three years in the form of a reduced expenditure ceiling. The ceiling itself may be raised or lowered by a simple majority vote of taxpayers in any jurisdiction. None of these procedures has yet been used, and it is impossible to know if regular use will be made of them in the future.

In jurisdictions where the limitations are statutory not constitutional, provisions for formal escape are less certain. In New Jersey, up to 3 percent of appropriations may be excluded from the limit according to ordinance procedures, but it is unclear what would happen above that limit. Local governments can exceed the limit by referendum and may make use of the 3 percent emergency appropriation with permission of the State Board of Local Finance.[14] In Colorado, no provision has been made for formal escape, without presumably repealing or amending the statute in the regular way. Lack of an emergency provision has been criticized as increasing the rigidity of the limitation, since the only legitimate way of funding an emergency outside the limit would be to change the whole statute. Otherwise internal transfers of funds would have to be made by emergency authority of the governor, and such transfers would presumably necessitate later supplementals to make up the shortfall. So far no attempts at amendment or circumvention in this way have been attempted.

When Is an Expenditure Not an Expenditure?

One of the biggest headaches in implementing expenditure limitations is trying to decide what is to be counted as expenditure so that it will come under the limitation. Whatever categories are excluded from the definition will automatically attract spending. Everything depends on the wording of the limitation and how it is interpreted.

For those jurisdictions where the limitation applies only to the general fund the motto for those running into pressure is straightforward: create a new fund. County budgeters in Arizona, who have had plenty of practice at this one since 1928, have made an art of it. By now about half of the amount in county budgets is exempt from limitation. Sometimes county authorities have gained statutory exemption by appeal to the legislature; sometimes the new fund has relied on opinions of the state attorney general; sometimes counties have just gone ahead on their own. For example, counties are obligated by state mandate to pay the employers' costs for teachers' pensions, a cost impossible for school districts to support, since it escalates with rising salaries and is beyond county control. The answer is the Teachers' Retirement Fund, which by tacit agreement is not subject to the county expenditure limitation. Other exempt funds include the Road Fund, the Health Services Fund, the Public Works Reserve Fund, the Auto License Fund, the Federal Revenue Sharing Fund, the Anti-Recession Fiscal Assistance Fund, and various specific grants funds. In addition there are a whole host of exclusions, including air pollution, cemeteries and indigent health costs, war emergency, TB control, and superior court costs.

In Colorado, about half of the budget is financed through the general fund, and hence is subject to limitation. There is a continual drift toward cash funding, and a reliance on these cash funds. Previously, the unspent portions of such funds were allowed to revert to the general fund. Social services, Medicaid, and developmental disabilities, for example, now segregate federal dollars and ensure that these are spent rather than mingled with the general fund. Managerial service, which does consulting for other agencies, is now entirely self-financing and thus is outside of the general fund limit. Institutions of higher education now ensure that all tuition income is spent rather than returned to the general fund as previously. Though these examples may seem in the nature of accounting detail, they are important in diminishing the amount under the general fund. Some agencies are in a better position to undertake cash financing than others. The Department of Natural Resources, for example, has made a serious attempt to refinance its activities by fees and by extracting parts of federal financing, such as program overhead allocations, which had previously gone to the general fund. The department is also attempting to gain statutory exemption for fees, such as mine and dam inspection fees, which currently go into the general fund. Most agencies have neither the fee-generating potential nor the political suppor. to enable them to achieve similar independence.

Despite the attempts of other states to avoid restricting limitation to the general fund, wording of the amendments may be ambiguous enough to cause trouble. In Arizona, expenditure has been defined according to its appropriation from state tax revenues. Federal funds are clearly excluded and the amendment has been interpreted to exclude income from interest, sales, and services. The problem has been that many services are financed from funds containing a mixture of state tax revenues and other revenues, so that it has been necessary to examine every item of expenditure to determine whether it is financed by revenues classed as state tax revenue. Where doubts have arisen, the attorney general's opinion has been sought: Were fees and tuition of university students included as state tax revenue or were they revenue from sales and service? Is the share of state funds in federal projects, later reimbursed by the federal government, subject to the limit? Were premiums paid to the State Compensation Fund, which were used for expenditures for administration, settlements, and other purposes, to be included under the expenditure limitation? What about fines, forfeits, and penalties? In the end, it was estimated that 90 to 95 percent of total state expenditures came under the limitation, but presumably any interpretations of the attorney general could be challenged in the courts or by administrative action.

The Michigan amendment also tried to include total state revenues as a means of defining expenditure. Included under the limitation were appropriations from all general and special revenues listed in the Governor's Budget for 1978-79. Federal aid and the amount of any credits based on actual tax liabilities or the imputed tax components of rental payments were excluded. But credits not related to actual tax liabilities, such as the Home Heating Assistance Credit and the Higher Education Contribution Credit, were included. Several nonbudget items were also excluded, such as debt service funds, various state authorities, and trust and agency funds. These included the Michigan State Housing Development Authority, the Mackinaw Bridge Authority, and the Michigan Unemployment Compensation Trust Fund.[15] It is of course too early to see whether a proliferation of independent funds of this kind will spring up, or whether the exemption of debt service will lead to a greater volume of borrowing to finance government activities. In any case, new taxes and fees may replace the old ones currently listed in the 1978-79 Governor's Budget, and may thus escape the limitation.

In Tennessee, also, it was necessary to grapple with definition of "appropriation from state tax revenues." There the subcommittee of the Joint Finance Ways and Means Committee of the General Assembly, which was entrusted with drafting implementing legislation for the constitutional amendment, finally agreed that the distinction between tax and non-tax categories of revenues would have to be made arbitrarily.[16]

In California, expenditures include all local and State expenditures, funds to comply with court mandates, bond service payments, and revenues from fees and charges as long as these cover only the cost of the service they pay for. Some of these exemptions would seem to open large loopholes. For example, if a court order should be made to enforce lagging compliance with the *Serrano* school finance ruling, it could have the effect of exempting all educational expenditures from the limitation.

Ambiguous Limits

A number of problems have come to light in applying formulas relying on personal income as an economic indicator. Definition is obviously crucial, but the concept is by no means self-explanatory. In Michigan, for example, the amendment specifies that the definition of the United States Department of Commerce should be used, which avoids any ambiguity or local manipulation. But this solution involves the possibility that technical changes in the federal figures might have serious repercussions on state government expenditure. For example, the Senate Fiscal Agency has pointed out that figures for Michigan Personal Income for the past several years were recently revised downward by over 3 percent (over $2 billion in 1976). Had the amendment then been in effect, the revenue limit would suddenly have been $200 million tighter, "due to a technical change in Washington, D.C. rather than an economic change in Michigan." [17]

At least in Michigan, a set figure for the past year will be used. In Arizona, a calculation has to be made for the *forthcoming* fiscal year. For this purpose a special commission has been set, which must come up with estimates of personal income in October and February while the budget is being developed. Its final and binding estimate is made in April, very near the end of the budget process, which is usually finished toward the end of May or beginning of June. In other words, while the budget is being worked on in the executive branch, and during the early debates in the legislature, no one really knows just what the limit will be.

In Tennessee and other states following its model, the situation is more flexible. The legislature is empowered to decide on the economic indicator it wants, and is presumably empowered to change it at will. But Tennessee has had to cope with another problem. In limiting the growth in state government expenditures to the growth in personal income, it could have taken two alternative paths. One was to use a year-by-year approach, looking only at the percentage growth for a single year at a time. The second approach was to establish a base year and run an index from it, allowing state expenditure to keep up with the index for personal income in the state. Thus, if appropriations fell below the index in any one year, they could "catch up" in later years. This latter approach was adopted. Less conservative than the year-by-year approach, it yields greater room for maneuver. [18] In California, similarly, an authority may keep its base intact even if it spends less than the limit in any one year.

Playing With Surpluses

One of the main ideas behind expenditure limitation has been that taxes would be reduced or surpluses would be returned to the people. This idea is less straightforward than it looks. Clearly the intent of the limitations would be negated if states raised more money than they needed and then kept it in the bank instead of spending it. The amendments in Michigan and Arizona, by defining the expenditure limit according to a revenue limit, have hoped to avoid this problem by preventing the raising of excess revenues in the first place. Still the possibility exists, given uncertainty in revenue forecasting (quite apart from the uncertainties in calculating the limit) that authorities will slip and will raise more than they need. In Arizona, the matter is dealt with by carrying the surplus over to the next year where it is counted in the limitation. Any tax relief counts as ordinary expenditure. In Michigan, if the surplus for any year reaches more than 1 percent of the revenue limit, the excess revenues must be rebated to the taxpayers on a pro rata basis according to personal income tax and single business tax returns. Obviously a lot of people who contributed other taxes to the surplus will be left out, raising questions of fairness and equity. But what about a surplus below 1 percent? This *may* be transferred to the state budget and economic stabilization fund (for the use of which no procedure is set out), *or* rebated to the taxpayer, *or* carried over to the next year where it will be *added* to the expenditure limit. In other words, a government that plays its cards right, keeping an annual surplus of just below 1 percent, will be able effectively to extend its expenditure and also its expenditure base by that amount.

In California, the problem of reserves relates to calculation of the size of base expenditures. If a state or local agency begins to set aside reserves in 1979-80, any future appropriations to augment these reserves would apparently not be subject to the expenditure limitation nor would any appropriations from them. It would therefore be possible to create a cache for future one-time expenditures. Furthermore, it is unclear whether the state surplus would count in the base year total, as the base includes emergency or contingency reserves as well as actual funds spent.

All of these procedures are still hypothetical, but the Colorado state government, which has experienced large surpluses above its expenditure limit, has used some of them for tax relief. The original statute mandated a reserve of 4 percent of revenues for property tax relief. This section has now been amended to 4 percent of general fund appropriations for the current fiscal year to be used for tax relief in general. In the last two years, several tax relief measures have been passed, including indexing the income tax, repealing food and home heating sales taxes, repealing gift and inheritance taxes, and reducing business and income taxes. This still has left an embarrassingly large surplus of over $300 million out of a general fund of about $1.5 billion in 1979-80. Some of this surplus has also been used for tax relief, but in a rather more novel way. An amount was allocated to schools, on the argument that unless the state stepped in, property taxes would have to be raised. Similar appropriations have been made to highways, water projects, and municipal pensions, which would otherwise have entailed gasoline, sales, or property tax increases at the local level. None of these amounts comes under the general fund limitation. According to current revenue estimates, it is unlikely that revenue surpluses will diminish substantially in the next few years, and allocations from them have been budgeted for the future.

The Problems of Earmarked Funds

It has been the practice for many years to earmark certain revenues for particular expenditures. The most familiar example is gasoline taxes earmarked for highways. If these earmarked funds are placed outside the limit, as in a general fund limitation, they provide an easy means of evasion. New Jersey, for example, has earmarked casino revenues specifically for the aged and handicapped. Even if earmarked funds are included in the general fund, it is possible to argue that they can be diverted before they reach it, so that they are exempted. For example, the Colorado legislature bought future flexibility in this way by making a loan to prison industries which would be repaid in future years when the repayments would not count as general fund revenues. It also set up a Utility Contingency Reserve, which could only be spent the following year as a supplemental, when again it would fall outside the expenditure limit.

Other states have tried to close this loophole by ensuring that the earmarked funds fell under the limitation. Even so, problems can still arise. If, for example, an agency funded entirely by an earmarked source of revenue, such as a transportation department, finds that its revenues exceed the amount it is allowed to spend in one year, what should be done with the surplus, where legally it may be used for no other purpose? Conversely, what should happen if the earmarked revenues are declining relative to need, as in the case of gasoline taxes on a cents per gallon basis, and the agency finds it cannot spend up to its allocated limit? Should it accept a future responsibility to increase earmarked taxes, or subsidize the activity from general revenues, or should it always try to make things come out even by ensuring that expenditures and revenues balance in the earmarked fund? If so, it may be simpler to exempt the fund from the limitation altogether. In California, where this solution has in effect been adopted by exempting fees and user charges covering specific services, it appears that some leeway may be created by calculating amounts for overheads, contingencies, and depreciation within the payment scales.

Counting Time

Operating expenditures of government fit fairly easily within an expenditure limitation, because they are spent in the year for which they are appropriated. Capital construction, for which funds are appropriated for a number of years, is less easily dealt with. For example, in Arizona capital construction is financed through a Capital Outlay Stabilization Fund, funded through imputed rental payments from government agencies. It is still unclear whether outlays from this fund come under the expenditure limitation. Also in Arizona, problems arose when the legislature appropriated a large sum for prisons which would be spent over the next three to five years. Should the whole amount be counted under the limit in the year in which it was appropriated? Or should it be counted when it was spent? The decision of the attorney general was that if the legislature set up a timetable for expenditure of the sum, it could then be counted as it was spent. But if no timetable were set by the legislature, the money would count twice—once when it was appropriated and once when it was actually spent! [19] Further problems have arisen in cases where authorities are empowered to issue general obligation bonds, and where debt service, as in California, Michigan, and New Jersey is specifically exempted from the limit. Will governments come to rely overmuch on long-term debt financing in preference to taxation, even where the latter is more expensive? Or will restrictions on new borrowing contained in some amendments, combined with doubts about ability to repay under the limitations, lower bond ratings and make capital outlays more difficult and expensive?

Dumping Expenditures

Framers of many of the expenditure limitations were very conscious of the possibility that states might divest themselves of important expenditures and might mandate them on local governments. The existence or enactment of local expenditure limitations to some extent has prevented this practice. In New Jersey, however, the state was encouraged to aid local functions by exempting state aid from limitation. This exemption could function as a major loophole. In most other states, state aid to localities has definitely been placed within the limitation, and steps have been taken to ensure that state governments do not abuse their power to mandate functions.

Probably the most elaborate safeguards are contained in the Michigan amendment. The state may not reduce the state-financed proportion of the necessary costs of any *existing* activity or service required of local units of government by state law, and it may not require any *new* activity or service unless it pays for it (Section 29). Furthermore, the amendment requires that the proportion of total state spending paid to all units of local government shall not be reduced below the proportion in effect in fiscal year 1978-79 (Section 30). The intention is to prevent the state from reducing its share of the budget accruing to local authorities, but there are a number of problems in implementation. One difficulty relates to the timing of the sections. The amendment came into effect forty-five days after ratification, by which time several state mandates (including, for example, revision of the public health code, and water and air pollution quality control) had been passed but not yet implemented. It is unclear whether these would have to be reimbursed under the amendment. Several other problems relate to loose and vague wording. For example, regarding the "necessary" costs of local activities in Section 29, it could be argued that because certain costs are not a *necessary* part of an activity they could be reduced without infringing the amendment. Some difficulties may also arise with regard to federal mandates. If the federal government mandates expansion of an existing service or a new program on local government, is the state required to finance this under the revenue limit? Finally, the requirement that the current ratio of state contributions to local units must be maintained causes some difficulties, since it is not clear what the ratio refers to. State contributions currently include federal money, and there are many "gray areas where a payment may or may not actually be made to a specific unit of local government."[20]

Arizona has tried to close a similar loophole. Its amendment provides that if costs of a program are transferred from locality to state, the limitation may be increased by that proportion if revenues of the locality are reduced. But if the state transfers costs of a program to a locality, the state limitation must be reduced. The problem here seems to lie in defining a program. Does reclassification of certain highways from primary to secondary status, for example, which would place their maintenance under local authorities, constitute program transfer? In any case, the state shares certain revenues with local authorities, such as part of the income tax and sales tax. The local shares of these taxes are not covered by the expenditure limitation. It might thus be possible for the state to develop a new program, dump its administration on local government, and finance it through an increase in shared revenues.

Finally, Tennessee's provision looks almost too easy, since it provides that "no law of *general application* shall impose increased expenditure requirements on cities or counties unless the General Assembly shall provide that the state *share* in the cost" (emphasis added). This would appear to leave the way open for other kinds of laws or regulations to mandate expenditures, and might allow the state to share costs only marginally with local authorities.

THE LETTER AND THE SPIRIT

It is probably impossible to frame an amendment which cannot be evaded. Constitutions are made to be interpreted. Some of the implementation problems described here are perhaps inconsequential; some may be resolved by an authoritative decision or patched up with legislation. Some evasions are hypothetical and may never arise; others may answer deeper needs, where the limitation has prevented adequate carrying out of government services. Some, such as refinancing of functions through cash funds, may actually have desirable consequences; a few may reflect cynical manipulation and disregard of public responsibility. It is still too early to know how they will develop.

For the present, the letter of the law is being observed. Budgets have been below the limitations, leaving a margin for supplementals or revenue-estimating errors. Supplementals may be handled within the expenditure limit by consuming the margin, through reversions (i.e., reallocating unspent funds) or through transfers between line items. Cash flow problems are managed by monthly or quarterly expenditure schedules filed by the agencies. When agencies wish to spend, they issue vouchers paid by the central accounting authority, which can quickly check whether a spending allotment has been exceeded. Cases of illegality or deliberate overspending appear exceptional and are easily detected.

Continued compliance depends as much on the spirit of those carrying out the limitations as on their letter. The intent of the law is primarily to cut down government expenditure and reduce taxes, but it also implies that tasks can be carried out with fewer resources through greater efficiency, and that sharpened competition might result in better setting of priorities. It is difficult at this stage to assess such possible gains, both because of the newness of the measures and because some reforms would have taken place independent of them. The following impressions have been gleaned from interviews with officials in Colorado and Arizona, to whom I am greatly indebted for their time, patience, and cooperation.

There are considerable differences in opinion on the impact of the limitations. All agree that their future impact will be serious, but they are divided on their present effect. Many consider it marginal, despite an acknowledged loss of real spending power. Cuts can be taken care of by slack in the system—"Everyone buries a few contingencies"; "There's a contingency fund in every budget"; "This year we've been able to squirrel around . . . next year will be grim." Other officials worry about neglect of controlled maintenance as resources are concentrated exclusively on the operations side of estimates, about lack of current planning for expected population growth, and about side effects of accelerated economic development over the next few years.

The majority of officials stress the positive effect of the limitations on administration of resources, though some agencies are accused of being slow to catch on to the new situation and of continuing "to ask for the whole moon." One budget analyst reports that "the last budget allowed an increase of $72 million in spending for everybody, but they still asked for $76 million!" But in general there is agreement that agencies are learning to be more realistic and to understand that they have to live within the limit. The limitation is forcing a better priority system, and greater efforts must be made to justify requests. As an official in charge of budgeting for an agency explains: "Departments now have to frame questions so that they can learn what people want. It's no longer enough just to want to do good. When the pie isn't getting any bigger, someone has to deal with conflicting interests and the role of the official is to present the alternatives and force choice." An official in a state budget office also feels that heightened conflict indirectly brings about better justification for estimates: "I'm not worried about you and you're not worried about me, but when we get ready to air our case, we have a better justification." Managers and executives can no longer simply go on doing what they have always been doing but must stop and reassess their activities.

Yet some administrators warn of less beneficial consequences. "Sure," says one budget official, "the limitation makes budgeting easier. All you have to do is implement a general economy policy. But it's a cop-out as far as the real needs are concerned. It gives the people at the center the illusion they are managing everything, that they are omnipotent, while the real problems aren't being dealt with." Similar unease is expressed by a top agency official, who considers that the limitations have tightened certainty and enhanced executive leadership but have carried the danger of substituting a top-down arbitrary process for the previous arbitrary bottom-up one. Presumably a limitation is imposed so the center does not have to decide each and every issue on the composition of the total.

Several officials believe the limitations have had a positive effect on legislators, lending some much needed discipline to the budgetary process in the legislature. They cite consolidation of supplementals, limitation of pork-barrel trade-offs, shortening of the budget passage, and prevention of automatic expenditure increases, though these are also connected with factors such as changed political balance in the legislatures. But there are a number of complaints that the legislature is taking on a management role and concentrating on a lower level of detail to the detriment of the real issues, of which they are alleged to display little knowledge and less understanding. Some fear is expressed that officials will spend more time and energy on lobbying for political support, building constituencies, and "packaging" their programs for the best appeal, as opposed to actually doing the work. In the short run, the agencies with the biggest and most powerful constituencies will probably gain ground from the limitations, while others would lose out.

Because of the newness of expenditure limitations, it is premature to judge their effects. It is hard to separate them from a general mood of fiscal conservatism which is affecting budgeting even in jurisdictions that have not enacted them. We do not know whether the preliminary difficulties of implementation discussed here are merely birthpangs, to be forgotten as the healthy child emerges, or whether they are precursors of much more serious problems as constraints tighten and public needs grow. Nor do we know whether, after an initial jolt, officials will use their energies not to do a better job with fewer resources but to refine evasion techniques.

To what extent might federal proposals for constitutional expenditure limitation, if passed, encounter similar problems to those of the states? Clearly much depends on the exact wording of the limitation and the determination of politicians and officials to evade it. The framers of both the long and short amendments discussed in this book have tried to foresee future implementation problems and to make provision for them. Their solutions differ in three main respects from those so far adopted in the states.

First, the use of GNP for the calendar year preceding the fiscal year should ease problems in calculating the expenditure limit. Because the measure is well established and fairly unambiguous, and because it would be well known in advance of the budget period, problems of uncertainty relating to concepts of personal income or current year estimates would be avoided. There also appears to be a clear intention of year-to-year calculation, as opposed to an economic index basis. Second, the application of any surplus revenue to reduction of the public debt in the long amendment deals with the problem of the government raising more tax revenue than it needs without becoming involved in rebate schemes.

The short amendment makes no provision for surplus revenues and leaves open the possibility of accumulation of reserves. Third, since the federal government does not receive grants from other governments, there is no need to exempt such revenue from limitation.

In other respects, the federal amendments are likely to encounter similar problems to those of the states. First, the emergency provision for overriding the limit resembles most closely that of Michigan, requiring statement of emergency by the executive and a two-thirds majority vote by both houses of the legislature. The change of the limit itself by three-fourths of both houses of the legislature and by a majority of state legislatures in the long amendment is unparalleled in the state provisions. Since none of the emergency provisions have yet been used, there is no way of knowing whether the federal provisions will provide a significant loophole. Second, it is unlikely that all problems regarding definition of expenditures have been solved, though the framers of the amendments have avoided the difficulties experienced by states that limited only general fund expenditures. The use of the word "outlays" rather than "appropriations," as used in state provisions, is obviously intended to be inclusive. It would seem to cover expenditures only as they were spent, so that long-term appropriations could be made with only current expenditures being counted under the limitation. It is unclear whether "tax relief" would count under the limitation. Third, the federal amendments have tried to prevent the federal government either from exempting grants to state and local governments from the limitation, or from mandating new or expanded activities on them. Again, much depends on interpretation of wording, that is, the distinction between "redefinition or classification" and "new or expanded." It is also unclear what constitutes a state or local government, or whether federal court mandates are included in the prohibition. Finally, the federal proposals would be likely to encounter problems similar to the states' relating to any earmarked funds.

All these problems of implementation arise from questions of interpretation. It is impossible to close every potential loophole or to foresee in detail all potential problems. Whether the limitation would be enforced would depend in the last resort not so much on its wording, but on the degree to which it hampers the objectives of those subject to it, the belief it engenders that it is beneficial in its results, and the willingness of those who apply it to abide by its spirit.

Appendix D

DEVELOPMENT OF IDEAS ABOUT
BALANCED BUDGETS

Carolyn C. Webber

THE IDEA OF a balanced budget for government is a relative new-comer in the long history of ideas; it gained legitimacy only about one-hundred years ago. By the middle of the nineteenth century, governments of European nations were preparing regular, periodic estimates of anticipated expenses, and then were submitting these expenses to legislatures, both to get approval and to authorize funding so the bills could be paid. Legislative authorization of expenditure and legislative approval of taxes and debt became the instrument for maintaining the rough equivalence between income and outgo that is the essence of balanced budgeting. The point was simple: like a prudent individual, government should not spend beyond its means.

Simple, perhaps, but long in emerging and even longer in gaining acceptance. The balanced budget idea did not spring full-blown from some nineteenth century bureaucrat's brow; it rested on a long chain of ideas and technical innovations. To examine their evolution it is helpful to separate the composite idea—balanced budget—into its technical and normative components, tracing the development of each. And because balanced budgets result from interactions among spending, taxes, and debt, it is also helpful to examine the development of these aspects of government financial policy.

Governments had the technical capacity to keep accounts long before they learned to make budgets. Among the cuneiform tablets and papyri surviving from ancient civilizations in the Middle East, archeologists have deciphered tabulations of taxes received in money or kind. The Athenians during the golden age of Pericles (in the fourth century B.C.) also kept records of spending; we know this because the accounts were chiseled into stone and then set into the walls of the treasury on the Acropolis. The Romans, too, maintained registers of receipts and expenditures. But since their scribes wrote on wax tablets, not clay or stone, we know of them only indirectly—from the observations of critics like Pliny the Elder or Cato the Censor. Some historians have called the accounts of the early Roman Empire's various treasuries* "budgets," but it is a virtual certainty that these were only more comprehensive accounts than government had maintained before that time. Parchment tax rolls still survive from medieval England; the famous Domesday Book was a comprehensive survey of land, landowners, and the fiscal obligations associated with each landholding. Even the Incas, who never invented written language, kept tax registers with a kind of fiscal macrame, complex patterns of knots tied into string. When one considers the problems that must have been involved in maintaining these records in societies in which tiny segments of their populations were literate, and when men could move from place to place only on foot or by oar or sail, any capacity to maintain records of taxes and spending, however limited, is impressive. But because taxing and spending have always been among the most critical businesses of governments, organizations and methods for keeping track of finances emerged simultaneously with government itself.

The purpose of early governments' financial records was not, as at present, to know where government and the economy were going; ideas about futurity and management emerged many centuries later. Ancient, medieval, and some early-modern government accounts were a series of undifferentiated line-item entries, seldom added up, and hard to decipher because they were kept in paragraph form. Their primary purpose was not synthesis but con-

---

*The *Aerarium, Aerarium Militare,* and the *Fiscii.*

trol of delinquent taxpayers and dishonest collectors. If a taxpayer failed to pay up, if a collector or official put his hand in the till, the records sometimes made it possible to identify a culprit so government could take action against him.

Before the modern era governments seldom had adequate resources. Except for the great empires of world history whose wealth derived from extorting tribute from conquered people, governments were poor. Without machine technology, production was limited and most people lived at subsistence levels; their poverty established a ceiling on amounts kings could command in taxes and rents. The difficulty of getting from place to place, moreover, while consonant with the leisurely tempo of agricultural society, meant that financial administration would be decentralized whether rulers wished it or not. Tax collectors operated with autonomy and maintained their own timetables. Provincial tax proceeds came in slowly; months, sometimes years, elapsed between collection and remission.

Meanwhile, costs of government accumulated. Without revenue, kings and their finance ministers had to worry about how they would meet current expenses. Even royalty could not put off creditors indefinitely; eventually they would stop providing supplies. But rulers could often manage to remain solvent by improvising, and they invoked the same strategies time after time. They sold patrimonial land for cash, or they debased the currency. They granted privileges in exchange for cash payments, and they permitted liberties not previously allowed in exchange for new taxes with yields that might be more certain and perhaps easier to collect. If the situation were truly desperate, they sold jewels or they borrowed money, pledging gems, royal land, or anticipated tax receipts as security for loans.

Like modern developing nations with deficient revenue, governments before the modern era borrowed from private sources. They developed working relationships with a succession of lenders, medieval and renaissance equivalents of Citibank or Chase-Manhattan—the Knights Templars in Paris, and the banks owned by the Bardi and Peruzzi families in Florence, and Flemish bankers in Bruges and Antwerp. When pre-modern governments borrowed from private lenders, jockeying for mutual advantage established conditions for their loans; when finances were strained they offered trade concessions, monopolies, and tax-collection franchises as loan inducements. As the international banks now do when they lend to states like Turkey, Peru, or Zaire, medieval and renaissance bankers risked loss of interest and principal from default caused by internal instability. But like the international banks, they continued to lend because the terms were profitable. Premodern governments often defaulted on and abrogated loans, bankrupting lenders. Bankers thus felt justified in commanding higher interest rates from governments than from any private borrowers; when governments had no other options, they paid through the nose.

In the seventeenth century, economic growth was creating a reservoir of funds seeking safe and profitable investment. Several states with growing mercantile economies tried to tap into it to reduce borrowing costs; they established banks in order to underwrite government debt and sell it to the public. Because bonds issued by public banks bore legislative guarantee, investors were willing to buy them. But, since governments had maintained bad credit ratings for so many centuries, the market was wary; investors would not buy government debt except on the most favorable terms. To sell their earliest issuances, public authorities had to offer very long term bonds paying interest at more than the going market rates.

With accumulating experience in public capital markets, governments became more reliable creditors and, as a consequence, their interest cost for new loans declined. State financial managers developed schemes for reducing the carrying costs of the public debt by buying up outstanding bonds issued at rates higher than those currently being offered. Reacting to the disastrous inflation and subsequent collapse in value of stock in the South Sea Company (chartered by the English crown in 1714 in its first effort to reduce borrowing costs by consolidating debt), Robert Walpole, a mid-eighteenth century finance minister, invented a new and better method of refunding. He established a special account in the treasury, calling it a sinking fund. If government regularly reserved any surplus, invested it in government securities, and then set aside accrued interest in the sinking fund, it could, in principle, pay off debt painlessly and automatically. The scheme did not work out quite as Walpole expected, largely because the high costs of wars were not covered by tax receipts. After armies were paid, not only was there no money left to retire debt, there was need for new borrowing.

But the idea of a sinking fund survived nonetheless; during the nineteenth century it was to become one of the means employed to attain balanced budgets.

But that's getting ahead of the story. By the late eighteenth century, a number of strains of development were coming together to create the idea of a budgeting function in government. One of them related to the kinds of taxes governments collected and to the ways these taxes were administered. From the earliest times, governments had levied taxes on consumption—import and export duties and internal imposts on a few food staples and on luxuries. During the sixteenth, seventeenth, and eighteenth centuries, European nations had tried to meet rising expenses by adding new consumption taxes a few at a time; by the late eighteenth century there were literally hundreds of market taxes. With economies growing and incomes rising, the taxes should have been productive. Yet governments still faced chronic fiscal crisis.

Governments were always short of funds, largely because the myriad taxes were administered in disorganized ways. Governments discharged most expenses with revenues earmarked for specific purposes. For each tax or related group of taxes government factored out administration to a fund—an independent organization authorized to collect the tax and then pay out receipts for its designated purpose. Like some independent authorities of the modern world (the Social Security Trust Fund, the Federal Reserve Banks) fund officials were virtually autonomous. Although large sums might pass through their hands, governments had no means of compelling fund officials to report regularly on receipts, expenditures, and balances, or to remit outstanding balances if a surplus remained. If officials reported information about tax receipts and spending to the center, it was long after the fact—as much as twenty, thirty, or even eighty years. Even with the lackadaisical pace of government in those days this was, of course, far too late to make any use of it. But if the information came in sooner, governments were not much better off. Officials at the center could then know how much had been spent and received by each fund in prior periods, but there were no workable techniques for deriving information about totals.

When governments began to borrow large sums from the public, comprehensive, systematic, and above all, timely records of tax receipts and spending were required. Unless government could demonstrate its capacity to service and redeem the public debt, no one would buy its notes and bonds. In the fourteenth century, city fathers in the city-states of northern Italy had made that discovery. Just as Italian merchants pioneered the use of double-entry book-keeping for private business, so too, communal governments in Italy were the first to develop current tax and expenditure accounts for use in funding their debt. By the last quarter of the seventeenth century, central governments in England and Prussia were main-taining systematic records of past receipts and spending by their various funds. Pressure from the center on fund officials (threats of fines and imprisonment) enforced reporting on a reasonably cur-rent basis—within six or nine months after accounts for each period had been closed. Central government could then use information about prior period receipts and spending by each fund to determine whether new taxes and borrowing would be needed for any given purpose in the next period.

Although seventeenth and eighteenth century governments were minuscule by modern standards, their need for money kept rising, mainly because of large expenses for wars. Between 1760 and 1815, European nations were at war with each other and with their over-seas colonies about two-thirds of the time. Like modern nations, they financed war by taxing and borrowing. But fiscal management with the earmarking method was difficult because there was no way of shifting from one use to another. If fund expenses were not cov-ered by receipts, governments had only two options, to add on new taxes or to borrow. Usually they did both. When expenses went up they imposed new taxes. And like New York City before its fiscal crisis of 1975, eighteenth century governments borrowed so heavily that in any given year a large proportion of tax receipts—some-times as much as two-thirds of the total—was committed ahead of time for debt service.

The consolidated fund idea is a culmination of all these develop-mental steps that created techniques necessary for budget making. Until the beginning of the nineteenth century, government financial officials had no verifiable knowledge of total receipts and expendi-tures. Although the various branches of civil government and the military might (and as the century passed, often did) report receipts and spending to the top, governments had no procedures for add-ing them all up. Without a formal process of synthesis, it was hard to think about achieving equivalence between income and spending

—between taxes and debt on one side, and spending on the other. The consolidated fund idea provided the vital technique for relating spending to taxes and debt. It is a critical component of accumulating budgeting technology. First proposed for England in the 1770s, it was adopted in the 1780s and became fully operational early in the Napoleonic Wars. By that time, too, France and Prussia were using consolidated accounts to determine future spending needs.

Over the next sixty years, governments built effective structures for administering taxing and spending. By a series of discrete changes, governments required spending departments to submit accounts at regular intervals, at first once each year and then quarterly. Departmental autonomy slowly was constrained as governments mandated the same fiscal year for all departments, and uniform accounting methods within each one. Neither totals nor comparisons between departments were meaningful when each department opened and closed books on a different date, and when some departments reported total appropriations whether or not all funds had been spent, while others accounted only for money actually paid out. Eventually governments prohibited departments from spending money appropriated for one purpose on some other, enforcing the restriction by subjecting each department to a post-audit of receipts and spending. Accretion of all these techniques not only provided means for making budgets but gave governments control devices for limiting spending.

While budgeting rests on all these technical components, there is a large normative element as well. It was (and perhaps still is) conventional wisdom that making a plan for spending and sticking to it demonstrates moral rectitude—a capacity for disciplined restraint. Objections to the swollen, deficit-ridden budgets of the past decade stem, in part, from a conviction, deepseated in our fiscal culture, that unbalanced budgets are intrinsically bad; as the foremost nineteenth-century advocate of balanced budgets for government put it, "a great political, and above all, a great moral evil." Because the present debate over balanced budgets is shot through with moralistic overtones, it is important to explore the origin and evolution of the values implicit in ideas about balance when related to budgets so we may learn how some of us have come to think as we do.

The normative component of balanced budget ideology derives from ideas generated during the great eighteenth century intellectual revolution we now call the French and English Enlightenment.

Balance was one of the grand organizing ideas in eighteenth century thought. It derives from Newton's theories of a stable and orderly universe. Political and moral philosophers of that age, men like Locke, Hume, Bentham, and Adam Smith, modified Newton's cosmology to build a new organizing model for government and the economy. If, as Newton postulated, a universal force controls the motion of objects on earth and of the tides, and maintains the planets in stable orbits, checking their tendency either to fall into the sun or to fly off into space, balance must be the organizing principle for social relations as well. Newton's theories demonstrated convincingly to these theorists that God or Nature (they used the terms interchangeably) had ordained universal balance and order. But in relations among men on earth, things had somehow gone awry. Because government had enforced all kinds of constraints on relationships, God's balancing force had not operated freely. It was therefore modern man's task to restore the order God intended by giving government, the economy, and society a gentle nudge in the right direction.

The solution, they postulated, was a political and economic system that operated under minimal rules. States could best be governed by dividing power among an executive and a representative legislature that would itself manifest a balance among various elements of society. Economic order could best be achieved by limiting state interference in markets. Without regulation, individual decisions of buyers and sellers would balance out to achieve the best possible outcome—low prices for buyers, and high output and high profits for sellers. Equivalence or proportionality among the parts would then, as in Newton's cosmos, automatically result in a stable system in which disparate elements would coexist in harmony.

By the time the technique for making and enforcing budgets had accumulated, balanced budgets were perceived by the public to be both virtuous and eminently desirable. The question, then, is how the values implicit in abstract ideas about balance came to be tied to the technique of budget making to produce the composite idea of a balanced budget. At the most abstract level, an answer lies in interactions among balance conceptions and two other seminal formulations of eighteenth century thought: those of efficiency and rationality. Following Hume's psychological theories, enlightenment thinkers believed profoundly in man's capacity to improve his environment through exercise of his God-given superior intelligence. Deriving their ideas from personal observation of how government operated, and then drawing parallels between government and the methods of empirical science, men like the Scottish economist, Adam Smith, the English chemist, Joseph Priestley, and the French engineer, Jean Vauban, suggested that, even within the minimal government they wished to see, performance of tasks essential for its operation would be improved and costs reduced by changing its internal organization. Since each of these eminent men had either worked in or served as advisor to his own government, their criticism of its administration could not be dismissed as the faultfinding of some crank.

In a changing environment, their ideas fell on fertile ground. Centralization, consolidation, and cost cutting became guiding principles and goals of administrative reforms in nineteenth century governments. During the early years of the century, governments began to build new style bureaucracies that employed the latest methods and were committed to saving money through efficient operation. Balanced budgets were at once a *means* for emergence of modern bureaucracies, and an important developmental *goal*.

Given the prior existence of necessary technology, the immediate impetus for proliferation of balanced budget ideas came from widespread public reaction against the heavy taxation all European governments had imposed, and the extensive borrowing they had engaged in to pay for the Napoleonic Wars. In each nation, and in all walks of life, citizens agreed that the burdens had been excessive. When peace finally arrived in 1815 there was an immediate wave of retrenchment. Legislatures voted to strike special war taxes from the books. In England, where an income tax—viewed by policymakers as necessary, but nevertheless, universally hated—had been imposed continuously from 1802 on, an act of symbolic repudiation celebrated its repeal. To demonstrate its intention of getting rid of the income tax permanently, Parliament ordered that all records associated with it be burned in a public bonfire.

Then they confronted the problem of debt, for the wars had been supported mainly by deficit financing. Between 1795 and 1815 England's outstanding debt had quadrupled, Austria's had multiplied five times, and all other nations had expanded their borrowing beyond precedent. Nineteenth century legislatures, reflecting the increasing influence of mercantile and manufacturing interests, viewed a large public debt as a handicap. Long before neo-Keynesians had noted the "crowding out" effects of large-scale government borrowing, early nineteenth century entrepreneurs had realized that, if governments entered the market for capital, their superior credit worthiness would soak up all funds seeking investment, leaving nothing for private borrowers' needs.

By the early nineteenth century, moreover, the large international banking houses (Rothschild, Baring) had begun to function as governments' overseas debt-marketing agents. In an age of rising nationalism, mercantile and agricultural interests alike viewed foreign investment in public debt as a drain on national strength. Having internalized eighteenth century criticisms of governments' financial policies and organizational methods, nineteenth century legislatures were prepared to implement reforms. The financial policies they gradually evolved, and the organizational structures they designed to implement these policies, initiated systematic government budgeting. Along with the budgeting function came the beginnings of balanced budget ideology.

In our own time, everyone knows that balanced budgets result from an equivalence between taxing and borrowing on one side of the budgetary equation, and spending, debt service, and debt retirement on the other. In the nineteenth century this assertion was not the truism it has since become, for governments had to devise techniques for making budgets, then had to find resources for keeping them in balance. During the middle years of the century, as governments evolved the means for budget balancing, the rational methods of accumulated budgetary technology acquired a doctrinal rationale. With roots in normative principles of enlightenment philosophy—ideas about balance, efficiency, and effectiveness—nineteenth century budget doctrine crystalized around a few simple precepts. These have constituted the core of balanced budget ideology ever since: limit spending, tax lightly, maintain a surplus, borrow the minimum, pay off debt.

With its focus on moderation, balanced budget doctrine expresses the dominant values of mid-Victorian society in England where the ideas crystalized—sobriety, tranquility, and lack of excess. Before the doctrine had acquired the secular-religious connotation it was later to attain, it had found its head guru. This was William Ewart Gladstone, who was, intermittently between 1853 and 1885, Chancellor of the Exchequer and later Prime Minister and leader of the Liberal Party.

A charismatic figure, Gladstone had learned the lessons of the classical economists well; he believed the state should do the minimum possible and that its financial policies should reflect that intention. As Chancellor of the Exchequer and Prime Minister, his chief interest was financial policy. Even political opponents commended his "masterly knowledge" of budgetary intricacies. Before public policy statements were tailored to fit TV time slots, he held forth before Parliament on finance matters for four or five hours at a time and, if we are to believe his biographers, managed to maintain his audience's attention. His annual presentation of the budget manifested a knowledge of all aspects of finance; it combined a bookkeeper's zeal for detail with an understanding of aggregates. No department, division, or expense was too small to be a candidate for cuts as he hunted for economies. Accused of nitpicking not appropriate in a man of his stature, he defended his views:

Economy is the first and great article in my financial creed. I have felt for a considerable time that not only the actual scale of our expenditure but the prevailing temper of extravagance and the prospects it has opened to us have constituted a public inconvenience, and have threatened to become a public danger.

He was not rigid, but he tried to be consistent:

New wants are always coming forward, but where... provision is made for those new wants [it] ought to be... counterbalanced by new economies.

Economy was a matter of principle, not to be corrupted by political expediency.

No Chancellor of the Exchequer is worth his salt who makes his own popularity either his first consideration, or any consideration at all, in administering the public purse.... The Chancellor of the Exchequer is the trusted and confidential steward of the public. He is under sacred obligation with regard to all that he consents to spend.

In summary:

The Chancellor of the Exchequer should boldly uphold economy in detail; and it is the mark of a chicken-hearted Chancellor when he shrinks from upholding economy in detail, when because it is a question of only two or three thousand pounds, he says that it is no matter. He is ridiculed, no doubt, for what is called candle-ends and cheese-parings, but he is not worth his salt if he is not ready to save what are meant by candle-ends and cheese-parings in the cause of the country.

It was Gladstone, more than any other figure in nineteenth century governments, who promoted ideas and techniques of budget balancing, and he did so with the religious fervor of an evangelist. Because his views on governmental economizing provide the most complete statement of balanced budget ideology before or since, it is worth examining them with care. Perhaps it is because he was profoundly religious that he promoted his budget balancing convictions with such messianic intensity. Or perhaps, with his prolix Victorian style, the medium was the message. Spreading the gospel of economy was more than just a job; it was a moral obligation, a public duty, and always, a persistent struggle against implacable forces. He knew the right road to salvation, and, if he had his way, the nation would take it:

I do not believe there is any department of government in which it is more obligatory and more practical, than in finance, to resist evil in its beginnings. It is the duty of the Finance Minister . . . to lift up the warning voice, to exhibit the facts on which a right judgement must depend, and temperately to endeavor to lead the public mind to a healthier tone. The expenses of a war are the moral check which it has pleased the Almighty to impose upon the ambition and lust of conquest, that are inherent in so many nations. There is . . . glory and excitement about war, which, notwithstanding the miseries it entails, invests it with charms in the eyes of the community, and tends to blind men to those evils. . . . The necessity of meeting . . . the expenditure . . . it entails is a . . . wholesome check . . . making them . . . measure the cost of the benefits [that might result].

And yet, sometimes even a prophet gives vent to despair:

There has been a tendency to break down all . . . limits which restrain the amount of public charge. . . . I am . . . convinced that all . . . public expenditure beyond the legitimate wants of the country is not only a pecuniary waste . . . but a great political, and above all, a great moral evil. The mischiefs [of] financial prodigality . . . creep onwards with a noiseless and steady step . . . until they have reached a magnitude absolutely overwhelming . . . so large . . . that they seem to threaten the very foundations of national existence. . . . I trust that the day is come when a check is . . . put on the movement in this direction.

In mid-Victorian England, with its latent nationalism and changing political and social structure, it took more than exhortation to achieve a balanced budget. Financial policy must be made in accordance with principles. No matter what the pressures for spending might be at any moment, the "right and sound" method of financial management, Gladstone believed, was to maintain constant surplus. The way to achieve it was "to estimate Expenditure liberally.... Revenue carefully, make each year pay its own expenses, and take care [the] charge is not greater than...income." If a surplus is achieved it should be allocated to a sinking fund to pay off debt. Yet sometimes a general rule is not an adequate guide for policy decisions. In such instances, "Total Expenditure" should be the significant variable for maintaining the budget in balance: "the proper and necessary yearly expenditure is the Fixed Sum and Income ought to be adopted to meet that Expenditure." Establish a goal for spending, then levy taxes to meet it. While being always alert for possible economies, one should never lose sight of totals: "I do not think it unreasonable that government should look at totals as well as items."

But the items were important, for these were the real substance of spending. Although some aspects of the public debate over English fiscal policy in the 1850s and 1860s seems remote from interests of our own age, several of the controversies over items seems remarkably contemporary. Like the Congress in the 1970s, Victorian Parliaments liked to spend money, and, like Congress, they were divided into factions—spenders against savers, hawks against doves, traditionalists against innovators. Like our President, Gladstone believed in austerity; he deplored the spending faction's prodigal morality. The Conservatives under Disraeli, he once pronounced acidly, "have adopted a system of...making things pleasant all around.... Extravagance bubbles up everywhere." With a public penchant for spending, a surplus could become a path to perdition. Then, "the only security for a Chancellor of the Exchequer lies in his utter destitution. If he does not possess a surplus you cannot take it from him." His solution was simple: Limit income. "The most effective way of enforcing economy is to cut down income.... As long as you continue to levy the Income tax ...it will be vain to talk about effective and extensive economy."*

---

*The income tax was restored by the Liberal party in 1842 as a complement to its free trade policy.

What were some of the extravagant expenditures Gladstone lashed out against? Rearmament was the principal and most costly one. His moral strictures against war spending had been prompted by England's near defeat in the Crimea. Now money was needed to defend the nation's honor and its trade concessions in remote parts of the world (China, Abyssinia). France was a potential aggressor. The nation stood vulnerable because its weapons were old fashioned; it could defend itself only by investing in the latest technology. In tone and substance, the public debate over a scheme to fortify England's south coast against invasion from the sea, to buy a few ironclad warships, to replace muzzle-loading army rifles with automatics, is no different from present controversy over the respective merits, feasibilities, and costs of ECBMs and B-1 bombers, or Polaris and cruise missiles, or MIRVs. In the arguments over rearmament, Gladstone played the dual roles of saver and dove. His exchange of letters with Palmerston, the hawkish, free-spending Prime Minister when Gladstone served as Chancellor of the Exchequer, elaborates their differences:

> *Gladstone:* [I deplore] those maritime castles which we call a line of battle ships... which seem to be constructed on principles that aim at presenting as large a surface as possible to the destroying fire of an enemy.

> *Palmerston* (in reply): No doubt a full Exchequer is a good foundation for National Defense but... if the French had command of the sea they would soon find ways to make a full Exchequer empty.

On other issues Gladstone voiced the same concerns as a modern development economist. He understood that the nation's prosperity had resulted from increased productivity, and he believed that spending could rise along with GNP if the increase was not excessive.* He favored innovation if it improved the nation's competitive advantage, but believed that the private, not the public sector should bear the risk. In the early 1860s a business syndicate, proposing to lay a telegraph cable under the Atlantic, approached Pal-

---

*Statistical methods for measuring GNP were not developed until the present century, but policymakers were nonetheless thinking of economic growth in quantitative terms, for they often justified proposals for spending in terms of potential effect on a crude measure, National Wealth.

merston's government for a subsidy. Although he favored the cable, Gladstone objected to the subsidy on ideological grounds:

if the parties can cure themselves... of the vicious habit of looking for Government money... to overcome the difficulties of novel enterprises... knowledge... may bring capital forward freely without the great mischief of State intervention.

He did approve of spending for public education, for only a literate population could be entrusted with voting rights. (One of his great reform achievements was extension of the franchise to artisans and workingmen.)

If expenditure was adequately restricted, it could be supported by moderate taxes. Although some short-term borrowing would always be required to meet expenses before current revenue collections reached the Treasury, no long term loans should be needed. Government debt would remain fixed and might even decline while the budget stayed balanced.

During the mid-Victorian era the Liberal party implemented the classical economists' ideas about free trade. Without protective taxes on imports and penalties against exports, they had argued, nations could prosper through specialization. If each nation could produce products for which climate, resources, and skill endowed it with comparative advantage, all nations would benefit. Abolition of protective tariffs would expand markets; with rising production volume, costs would fall. Cost reduction would permit suppliers to reduce prices, further enlarging markets. Employment and income would rise, sustaining demand and maintaining prosperity.

The only problem the political figures who supported free trade policy could envisage was a need for *some* source of revenue. The Liberals had restored the income tax, intending that it serve as a temporary source of income to counterbalance deficits accrued from earlier borrowing. But even though the prosperity forecast by the classical economists came with free trade, it was never possible to do away with the income tax.

Gladstone favored the income tax as the revenue source least disruptive of economic relationships, but he always deplored the need to levy it. Nevertheless, as long as it was necessary, equity principles should govern its administration. Thus he supported increased exemptions for low-income taxpayers "whose affairs are so transparent they pay the tax fully and rigidly." And like some modern tax reformers, he wished to deny exemptions from income tax to charitable trusts on grounds that it promoted mismanagement of assets.

The history of ideas about taxes and budgets exposes a tendency for new creative approaches to difficult problems, once accepted and implemented, to degenerate into dogma, invoked mechanically. As for the ideology of balanced budgeting, it was all downhill after Gladstone, for those who followed after him in promoting the economic orthodoxy embodied in his ideas had little new to say. The substance of his arguments persisted in the rhetoric of budget balancers everywhere, for his was to be the most complete statement of conservative financial principles for governments. Until the 1940s, when Keynesian doctrine had legitimized deficit financing and permanent indebtedness, leading figures in and out of governments paid lip service to all the Gladstonian principles. Pronouncements favoring limited spending, moderate taxes, and debt retirement sounded a monotonous litany even as changing attitudes toward taxing and spending were bringing changes in practices.

The world was changing rapidly as the nineteenth century wore on. With large-scale industrialization and growth of mass markets, nations were becoming more interdependent; and they shared similar problems. At home, in all industrialized nations, political and social issues were both complicated and intractable. In England by the 1880s, the surpluses common in the 1860s and 1870s had disappeared; Gladstone's economizing morality was giving way to pressures for spending. There, as well as in industrialized nations such as Germany and Sweden, demands arose for governmental intervention to redress social inequity by putting a floor under incomes. With increased spending for education and old age insurance, plus the expense of a growing rivalry in armaments, the nominal taxation of the Victorian era no longer was sufficient to maintain budgets in balance.

Although Gladstone's rule of letting spending determine taxes still held on, increased spending mandated heavier taxes if budgets were to remain balanced. Between the mid-1890s and the beginning of World War I, many developed nations adopted some form of progressive income tax. With effective administration those taxes harvested the fruits of rapid economic growth; their revenues permitted governments to sustain spending, yet to maintain balanced budgets without heavy borrowing.

World War I changed all that, of course. A combination of massive borrowing and steeply graduated taxes on income and profits provided resources to fight it. But when the war ended, financial policymakers wanted nothing more than a return to orthodoxy. Warmed over Gladstonian ideas—minimum spending, moderate taxes, and debt retirement dominated their agenda.

Even depression-induced relief spending failed to shake the conviction that budgets should be balanced. Although England's expenditures rose steadily throughout the 1930s, the conventional viewpoint continued to reign; between 1931 and 1939 it had only one year with a deficit. In the United States, where social security spending had not yet been initiated, the federal budget ran a deficit in every year of the depression as unprecedented expenditure on imaginative new programs aimed to provide security and self-respect for the destitute. But even here, temporary improvement in 1934 and again in 1936 prompted Roosevelt (who always remained an economic conservative) to adopt a policy of reduced spending in an effort to bring the budget back into balance. Only the widespread hardship caused by massive unemployment led him to abandon it.

After World War II, with economies restored from the effects of war spending, with large latent demand, rapid population increase, rising productivity, and only moderate unemployment, governments could increase spending over pre-war levels while still maintaining balanced budgets; and they did. For a while, management of economies according to Keynesian principles promised to create the prosperous, rational societies all social reformers since the eighteenth century had dreamed of. If employment and incomes declined, so the argument ran, government should promote demand by taxing less and spending more. Depending on the size of the multiplier, the funds so generated would flow through economies in reverberating waves. Formulated during the depth of the depression, Keynes' theory contended that with large latent demand and no limit in factors of production, governments could maintain continuous expansion.

All Gladstone's rules were reversed. Governments spent more, taxed more, and borrowed more. As governments became the largest spending units in all the welfare-oriented nations of the developed world, budget deficits appeared, then grew larger each year.

And as government grew larger, the process of budget making changed in character. Given a large and diverse public sector, the problem was not how to limit spending, but how to make it easier. With many different programs aimed toward similar objectives, relationships between means and ends—between money in and products and services out—were not readily comprehended. Budget reform proposals of the 1960s and 1970s were attempts to develop techniques for improving the policymakers' and the public's understanding of spending, and to find better modes of management. Program budgeting and zero-base budgeting did not purport to limit government spending but to improve it. These proposals rested on value premises directly contrary to Gladstone's. Spending was not a great moral evil, but a necessary function of government, and, moreover, a pretty good thing at that.

The proposal to limit spending by means of constitutional amendment is interesting from a developmental perspective, for the balanced budget amendment, like the Constitution itself, reflects Enlightenment ideas, modified by nineteenth and twentieth century thought. Its major value premise holds that in budgeting balance is good and deficits are not. The technical device for achieving balanced budgets embodies the same automatic self-regulating principles as does the mechanism of the free competitive market in equilibrium postulated by classical and neo-classical economic theory.

The past century has witnessed an oscillating dialogue between spenders and savers. Spending interests have maintained dominance in recent years but the balance appears to be tipping back; once again there is public pressure for saving. While past events are a poor guide for predicting present and future outcomes, it is interesting that in the simple society of Victorian England, with its small government and moderate demand for social programs, efforts to limit spending were only partially successful. In his thirty-two years as architect of his country's financial policy, Gladstone managed to achieve a surplus in eleven years; spending equalled income in seven years; and for fifteen years the Treasury ran deficits (though by modern standards these were miniscule).

While ideas about spending limits are ideologically attractive, if a single-minded fanatic like Gladstone could not contain pressures for spending, will it be possible to do so now when demands on government from all sectors of society are so huge?

Notes

A Preface to Constitutional Expenditure Limitation:
Doing Together What We Cannot Do Alone

1. The sponsors were Senators John Heinz (Republican of Pennsylvania), and Richard Stone (Democrat of Florida) and the exact date was April 5, 1979. The amendment was patterned after an amendment prepared under the auspices of the National Tax Limitation Committee. The Heinz-Stone amendment leaves enforcement up to a Congressional enabling statute. The Senate amendment (SJ Res 56) was also introduced in the House (HJ Res) by Barber B. Conable (Republican, New York) and Ed Jenkins (Democrat, Georgia).

2. *National Journal,* "Lobbying Over the 1980 Budget—Can Congress Say No?," March 24, 1979, pp. 464-469. "If we cannot now do the job," says the Chairman of the House Budget Committee, Robert N. Giaimo, "then the American people, led by the balance-the-budget people, will impose a discipline on us that we refuse to impose on ourselves" (p. 464).

3. Plutarch, *Life of Pericles* (XII-XIV), quoted in Bruno D'Agostino, *Monuments of Civilization: Greece* (New York: Grosset & Dunlap, 1975).

4. Joseph Pechman, ed., *Setting National Priorities, The 1980 Budget* (Washington, D.C.: The Brookings Institution, 1979), pp. 26-27.

5. See *Nation's Business,* March 1979, p. 19.

6. For a discussion of programs of huge cost that slipped by see David R. Beam, "The Accidental Leviathan," *Intergovernmental Perspective,* V, 4 (Fall 1979), pp. 12-19.

7. James Tobin, "The Federal Budget and the Constitution," *Taxing and Spending,* 2, 4 (Fall 1979), p. 27.

8. Timothy B. Clark, "It's Back to the Drawing Board for Congressional Budget Cutters," *National Journal,* 11, 51-52 (22 December 1979), p. 2,148.

9. My favorite Washington gadfly writes, "If I proposed that for every percentage point that unemployment rises above, six or seven members of Congress, drawn at random, were declared impeached from office, you'd laugh." Oh, I might take my chances.

1. *Introduction: Progress and Public Policy*

1. For those who doubt the relative decline in defense spending, the following account is clear and convincing:

Federal government spending as a percentage of GNP has grown since the mid-1950s, from 17 percent in 1955 to 22.4 percent in 1977—or an increase of 31.8 percent. Since defense spending fell during that period from 9.6 percent of GNP to less than 5 percent, the real growth in the budget has come in non-defense spending (especially transfer payments)—which has grown from 7.5 to 17.4 percent. Here are the numbers at five-year intervals:

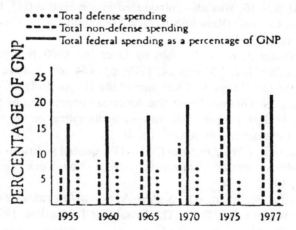

Source: The Economic Report of the President, 1978; in *Taxing and Spending* (February 1969), p. 15.

2. This section is based on my book, *Speaking Truth to Power* (Boston: Little, Brown & Co., 1979).

2. A Spending Limit As a Social Contract

1. This paragraph is drawn from my book, *Budgeting: A Comparative Theory of Budgetary Processes* (Boston: Little, Brown & Co., 1975).

2. The latest episode in this annual Perils of Pauline occurred early in April 1979, when Congress once again prevented the Government of the United States of America from defaulting on its obligatons. As usual, the hyperbole is exquisite: "The full consequences are impossible to predict and awesome to anticipate... Denigration of full faith and credit... incalculable effects... on the value of the dollar...." (W. Michael Blumenthal, Secretary of the Treasury), "For God's sake let's not destroy this nation... (Representative Parren Mitchell). The perennial last place team, still batting zero, had only the excuse of those nice guys who always finish last: "We are being blackmailed" (Representative Don Lungren), *Wall Street Journal* (3 April 1979), p. 3.

3. Constitution Making as Error Correction:
Why Defects in the Structure of Spending Were Not Evident Earlier in American History

1. W. U. Solberg, ed., *The Federal Convention and Formation of the Union of American States* (New York: Liberal Arts Press, 1958), p. 58.

2. Alexander Hamilton, John Jay, and James Madison, *The Federalist* (New York: Modern Library, 1937), pp. 60-61.

3. Robert A. Dahl and Edward H. Tufte, *Size and Democracy* (Stanford: Stanford University Press, 1973).

4. Samuel H. Beer, "In Search of a New Public Philosophy," in *The New American Political System,* ed. Anthony King (Washington, D.C.: American Enterprise Institute, 1978).

5. Hugh Heclo, "Issue Networks and the Executive Establishment," in *The New American Political System,* ed. Anthony King (Washington, D.C.: American Enterprise Institute, 1978).

6. For an empirical test of how "fair-shares" operates, see M. A. H. Dempster and Aaron Wildavsky, *The Political Economy of Public Spending* (forthcoming 1981).

7. Brian Barry, *Does Democracy Cause Inflation?*, Brookings Project on the Politics and Sociology of Global Inflation (September 1978), p. 53.

8. James M. Buchanan and Richard E. Wagner, *Democracy in Deficit: The Political Legacy of Lord Keynes* (New York: Academic Press, 1977), p. 125.

9. Ibid., p. 94.

10. This and the next three paragraphs are taken from the preface to the 3d edition of my book, *The Politics of the Budgetary Process* (Boston: Little, Brown & Co., 1979).

4. The Pogo Principle

1. Brian Barry, *Does Democracy Cause Inflation?*, University of Chicago, Brookings Project on the Politics and Sociology of Global Inflation (September 1978), pp. 34-35.

2. William A. Niskanen, *Bureaucracy and Representative Government* (Chicago: Aldine-Atherton, 1971).

3. On fiscal illusion, see Richard E. Wagner, "Revenue Structure, Fiscal Illusion and Budgetary Choice," 24 *Public Choice* (Spring 1976), pp. 45-61.

4. Bernard S. Frieden, *The Environmental Protection Hustle* (Cambridge: MIT Press, 1979).

5. Anthony Downs, "Why the Government Budget Is Too Small in a Democracy," XII, *World Politics* (July 1960), pp. 541-563.

6. John K. Galbraith, *The Affluent Society* (Boston: Houghton Mifflin, 1958).

7. Gordon Tulloch, "What Is to Be Done?," in Thomas E. Borcherding, ed., *Budgets and Bureaucrats: The Sources of Government Growth* (Durham: Duke University Press, 1977), p. 285.

8. William J. Baumol, "Macroeconomics of Unbalanced Growth: The Anatomy of the Urban Crisis," 57, *American Economic Review* (1967), pp. 415-426.

9. Work by Elinor Ostrom and her colleagues on police suggests that size leads to overspecialization, which results in a topheavy administration without equivalent increases in productivity. Thus small police forces keep as many men on patrol per unit of popula-

tion as the larger ones. See, for example, Elinor Ostrom and Roger B. Parks, "Suburban Police Departments: Too Many or Too Small?" in Louis H. Masotti and Jeffrey K. Hadden, eds., 7, *Urban Affairs Annual Review* (Beverly Hills, California: Sage, 1970), pp. 367-402.

10. See Aaron Wildavsky, *Speaking Truth to Power* (Boston: Little, Brown & Co., 1979).

11. William H. Riker, "The Cause of Public Growth," University of Rochester (1978), pp. 24-28.

12. Joel Haveman, *Congress and the Budget* (Bloomington of London: Indiana University Press, 1979).

5. Why Amending the Constitution is Essential to Achieving Self-Control Through Self-Limitation of Expenditure

1. Lochner v. New York, 198 U.S. 45, 75 (1904) (dissenting opinion).

2. Lawrence H. Tribe, "Issues Raised by Requesting Congress to Call to Constitutional Convention to Propose a Balanced Budget Amendment," Statement before the Committee on Ways and Means of the California State Assembly (11 February 1979).

3. See the excellent article by Kenneth W. Dam, "The American Fiscal Constitution," *The University of Chicago Law Review,* 44, 2 (Winter 1977), pp. 271-320.

4. This was the bargain behind the disastrous Public Expenditure Survey Committee (PESC) in Britain. See Hugh Heclo and Aaron Wildavsky, *The Private Government of Public Money,* 2d ed. (London: Macmillan Co., 1980).

5. Robert D. Behn, "The False Dawn of the Sunset Laws," *The Public Interest,* 49 (Fall 1977), pp. 103-118.

6. Since the President's budget is published around the same time as the State of the Union Message and the Economic Report, most new legislation will be reflected in the budget. Nevertheless, new legislation implying new spending keeps reappearing throughout the year. "In fiscal 1973, for example," Schultz and Dam report,

the President made 99 legislative proposals for new or expanded programs, only 45 of which were in the January budget. The other 44 emerged during the course of the year either in response to new problems or as an outlet for the fertile creativity of the federal bureaucracy.... To be sure, even the proposals that became law did not necessarily increase the budget because, though the legislation may have authorized expenditures, the appropriations may not have been forthcoming for another year. But many proposals involved back-door spending and generated increased expenditures immediately. Of the 99 presidential initiatives in the fiscal 1973 budget, 11 involved mandatory or back-door spending.

George P. Shultz and Kenneth W. Dam, *Economic Policy Beyond the Headlines* (New York: W. W. Norton & Co., 1977), p. 31.

7. *Wall Street Journal* (5 March 1979).

8. James M. Buchanan and Richard E. Wagner, *Democracy in Deficit: The Political Legacy of Lord Keynes* (New York: Academic Press, 1977), p. 176.

9. *The New York Times* (2 March 1979), p. A 11.

10. Jon Elster, *Logic and Society: Contradictions and Possible Worlds* (London: John Wiley and Sons, 1978).

11. Thomas C. Schelling, *The Strategy of Conflict* (Cambridge: Harvard University Press, 1960), p. 23.

6. *End Runs*

1. Robert W. Hartman and Joseph A. Pechman, "Issues in Budget Accounting," in Joseph A. Pechman, ed., *Setting National Priorities in the 1979 Budget* (Washington, D.C.: The Brookings Institution, 1979), p. 432. See also, Ibid. (1978), "Tax Expenditures," pp. 315-319.

2. The list of devices for loosening limits may be as large as the human imagination. On this one—governmental sales of services— I will let the Drafting Committee of the National Tax Limitation Committee speak in its own words:

With respect to sales of services, the consensus of the Drafting Committee is that such transactions represent voluntary relationships between the government and the people. As such, there is a presumption that these relationships reflect the individual's own determination that purchases of Federal goods and services offer to him a preferred alternative. Exclusion of the accompanying spending to satisfy such voluntary demands is consistent with effective limitation in two respects. First, Federal charges for such services must compete against alternative private suppliers of these same or comparable services. The ability of the Federal government to generate revenues in excess of the costs of providing the goods or services therefore is limited automatically by market forces. Second, inclusion of such spending within the Limit would subject other program outlays to the vicissitudes of private choice. Should the public's demand for such services increase faster than the increase in gross national product, other outlay programs would have to be reduced to stay within the Limit. This exclusion, however, does introduce the possibility that a Congress would attempt to subvert the Limit through the establishment of exclusive franchise entities. Operating without the discipline of competition, such entities would have implicit taxing powers with which to fund programs potentially beyond the reach of the Outlay limit. Whether adequate language can be drawn to preclude this possibility is problematical. Should it become a significant problem in the future, presumably support could be generated for an additional Constitutional amendment.

3. Hartman and Pechman, "Issues in Budget Accounting," *Setting National Priorities in the 1979 Budget,* p. 435.

4. I am indebted to Allan Schick's splendid paper "Constitutional Limitations on the Budget" (The Library of Congress, Congressional Research Service, Washington, D. C., 21 February 1979).

5. Murray L. Weidenbaum, *An Economic Analysis of the Federal Government's Credit Programs,* Center for the Study of American Business, Washington University, St. Louis (January 1977), p. 5.

6. Schick, "Constitutional Limitations on the Budget," p. 21.

7. Ibid., pp. 21-24. Schick continues:

If receipts sometimes are counted as negative expenditures, the opposite also has been true: expenditures are sometimes treated as negative receipts rather than as outlays of the federal government. The 1980 budget proposes to make direct payments to certain individuals whose wage increase are held to 7 percent or below. Some of these "wage insurance" payments are treated in the budget as refunds of tax receipts, not as outlays. The effect is to reduce outlays $2.3 billion below the total that would appear in the budget if such payments were computed as expenditures. A similar issue arose several years ago when the "earned income credit" program— direct payments to low-income workers—was established. The House and Senate Budget Committee wrangled for more than a year over whether earned income credits in excess of tax liabilities should be accounted for as offsets to receipts or as outlays. The compromise that was finally struck— treating existing credits as negative receipts but any additional ones as outlays—demonstrates the lack of hard and fast rules for these types of budgetary transactions.

8. Ibid., pp. 21-25.

9. Gerald E. Frug, "The Judicial Power of the Purse," 126, *University of Pennsylvania Law Review* (April 1978), pp. 768-769.

10. *Wall Street Journal* (4 April 1979), p. 20.

11. Since expenditure limitations at the state and local level do not appear to be entirely effective, to say the least, what gives me the idea experience at the federal level will be any better? So far as I know, all these are versions of requirements for a balanced budget. End runs essentially take three forms, at least two of which are not applicable to expenditure limitation. Balanced budgets bring in relationships on two sides—not only expenditures but also revenues, thus increasing by 100 percent the opportunity for obfuscation. Revenues may be overestimated in various ways that are irrelevant to a limitation that acts only on spending. States and localities also often have capital budgets that distinguish between investment in facilities with long life and current expenditures. This distinction is often blurred in practice. What is worse, shortages in current account may be made up by using monies in capital accounts. This is what got New York City into so much trouble. Fortunately, by omission or sheer inattentiveness, the federal government never got into capital budgeting. For a discussion of the evils of capital budgeting in a political climate, see Naomi Caiden and Aaron Wildavsky, *Planning and Budgeting in Poor Countries* (New York: Wiley, 1974).

7. Winners and Losers

1. *The Federal Convention,* ed. W. U. Solberg (New York: Liberal Arts Press, 1958), pp. 272-273.
2. The conservative view is expressed by Robert Bork of the Yale Law School, who served as Solicitor General under Republican President Gerald Ford:

Defense spending would have to compete under the outlay cap with rising costs of existing entitlement programs, such as Social Security, and these costs seem certain to soar even if no new programs are added. Defense is one of the few really discretionary items in the budget for any particular year, and the temptation will always be to meet the limit by deferring defense expenditures for one more year. Given Soviet attitudes and levels of military spending, far beyond their defense needs, delays in our defense spending could prove calamitous. The amendment's emergency clause is no safeguard because complex weapons systems require years of lead time. Unless the clause were routinely invoked, which is unlikely since it requires a declaration by the President and two-thirds vote of each house, by the time an emergency was perceived, it would be too late. [*The Wall Street Journal,* (4 April 1979), p. 20]

3. Charles E. Lindblom, *Politics and Markets* (New York: Basic Books, 1977).

4. For further discussion see my article, "Changing Forward versus Changing Back," a review of *Politics and Markets: The World's Political-Economic Systems,* by Charles E. Lindblom (New York: Basic Books, 1977), in *The Yale Law Review,* 88, 1 (November 1978), pp. 217-234.

5. David J. Ott and Attiat F. Ott, *Federal Budget Policy,* 3d ed. (Washington, D. C.: Brookings Institution, 1977), pp. 132-133, table 8-1.

6. See the preface to the 3d edition of my book *The Politics of the Budgetary Process* (Boston: Little, Brown & Co., 1979) for a more extended discussion of economic management and public spending.

7. In regard to the past, there is a volume in the making by Carolyn Webber and myself on *Taxation and Expenditure in World History.*

8. Murray L. Weidenbaum, *An Economic Analysis of the Federal Government's Credit Programs* (Center for the Study of American Business, Washington University, St. Louis, January 1977). For further discussion see Murray L. Weidenbaum and Robert DeFina, *The Cost of Federal Regulation of Economic Activity* (American Enterprise Institute, May 1978).

9. *Citibank Newsletter* (March 1978), p. 8.

Appendix C

1. In 1976 thirty-nine states had one or more constitutional restraints prohibiting an operating deficit, and eight others had one or more statutory restraints, leaving only Connecticut, Tennessee, and Vermont with none. Restrictions were of three kinds: (1) *Debt restrictions.* Twenty-five states had limitations on the amount or type of debt and eighteen had debt limitations of some kind; (2) *Balanced budget.* Twenty states required an appropriations act that does not exceed estimated revenues, and eighteen insist that the governor must submit a balanced budget to the legislature; (3) *Management of operating budgets.* Sixteen states required expenditures to be reduced if a shortfall in revenue were foreseen, and four others required that taxes be levied the following year to pay off

any year-end deficits. In practice, whether by constitution, statute, or custom, states do not undertake deficit-financing policies. State officials are unanimous that balanced budgets are a necessity, and states that do incur deficits take immediate action to wipe them out. (Council of State Governments, *Limitations on State Deficits* (RM577) Lexington, Kentucky, April 1976. See also A. James Heins, *Constitutional Restrictions against State Debt* (Madison: University of Wisconsin Press, 1963), pp. 7-9.

2. These could be circumvented where, as in counties in Arizona, the restriction was worded to apply to taxes "for general county operations." Where they were used for other purposes, the restriction would not apply. In any case, rise in property tax *assessments* effectively negated the rate limitation in some jurisdictions.

3. *Tax Expenditure Limitation Laws in New Jersey.* Comments by Richard F. Keevey, Assistant to the New Jersey State Budget Director, Southern Legislative Conference, Council of State Governments (July 27, 1976), Baltimore, Maryland, p. 1.

4. Advisory Commission on Intergovernmental Relations, *State Limitations on Local Taxes and Expenditures,* Washington, D.C. (February 1977), p. 2.

5. Standing Committee Report 66 of the Committee on Taxation and Finance (Hawaii), p. 11.

6. *Michigan's Tax-Expenditure Limit: Issues for Implementation,* Senate Fiscal Agency, Lansing, Michigan (February 1979), pp. 45-46.

7. *New Jersey State Budget, 1979-1980,* p. 14 b.

8. Constitution, Article IX, Section 26, quoted in *Michigan's Tax-Expenditure Limit,* op. cit., p. 2.

9. New Jersey has passed three budgets under its limitation statute (1977-78, 1978-80), and Colorado and Tennessee have passed two (1978-79, 1979-80). Arizona's budget for 1979-80, which began on July 1, 1979, is the first to be affected, while Michigan's 1979-80 budget, which will also be affected, starts on October 1, 1979. Hawaii and Texas, which work with biennial budgets, have not yet implemented any budget under expenditure limitation. The Gann amendment will affect the 1980-81 California state and local budgets.

10. *Proposition 13 Impact Reporter* (31 January 1979), p. 1.

11. A. Alan Post, "California's Fiscal Future," *Tax Revolt Digest* (July 1979), p. 1.

12. *Proposition 13 Impact Reporter* (29 June 1979), p. 3.

13. Barbara Haskew, *Implementing the Tennessee Spending Limit,* paper delivered at the Annual Meeting of the Western Economic Association, Las Vegas, Nevada (June 1979), p. 5.

14. In 1977, three municipalities requested voter approval to exceed the CAP and all were approved; in 1978, fourteen municipalities requested approval and only three were approved. In 1977, fifty-four municipalities and in 1978, 108 municipalities were excluded from the CAP because their municipal tax rate was less than ten cents. (*Tax Expenditure Limitation Laws in New Jersey,* op. cit., pp. 10-11.)

15. *Michigan's Tax Expenditure Limit,* op. cit., p. 25.

16. Haskew, op. cit., p. 6.

17. *Michigan's Tax Expenditure Limit,* op. cit., p. 4.

18. Haskew, op. cit., pp. 8-13.

19. The issue raised is whether the limitations are appropriations or expenditure limits. If the former, appropriations might be deliberately made for contingencies that would never arise, leaving surplus moneys in limbo indefinitely, or earning interest that by definition would not come under the limit. If the limits are expenditure limits, legislatures would be able to appropriate moneys over and above the limit in one year, preempting expenditures within the limit in future years.

20. *Michigan's Tax Expenditure Limit,* op. cit., p. 17.

Index